Ten
Questions
from the King

MARK CAHILL

Author of the bestselling books:
One Thing You Can't Do in Heaven, One Heartbeat Away,
The Watchmen, Paradise, Reunion, and *The Last Ride.*

WITH OVER 1.7 MILLION BOOKS IN PRINT
AROUND THE WORLD

"This is Mark Cahill's best book yet! It can motivate anyone of any age to witness to others. The stimulating questions throughout leave you thinking hard about how you are living your life. In Mark's inimitable and conversational style, the reader learns true-life evangelism by taking their cues from the way Jesus Himself interacted with the lost and the religiously proud. This book is one you don't want to miss."   — **Dennis H.**, *Carpenter*

"Wow! These challenging questions that Mark Cahill pitches to believers in Jesus Christ are like fast balls over the plate. I was both seriously engaged and encouraged as Mark presented his thoughts about evangelism, which are drawn from his studies of Jesus' interactions with the religious leaders, His disciples, and the common people during His world-changing ministry on Earth. Mark is a seasoned veteran at sharing the Gospel, and like a coach, he has a heart to train and strengthen fellow believers to reach the people around them for Jesus Christ. Mark's book is a real-world playbook to equip us for big-league evangelism. We gotta hustle! Time is short!"   — **Cindy H.**, *Promotional Sales*

"This book is the best book on evangelism that I have ever read! Its focus is to keep an eternal perspective with every soul you meet and in every conversation you have. The simplicity of that, in itself, is convicting. I'm excited to put these ten questions from the Master of evangelism into practice and to see His great work carried out."   — **Janet Z.**, *Admissions Registrar*

"Discipleship, Evangelism Training, and Faith Building are all rolled into this one book! Mark has used the premise of ten questions to challenge us all. As believers and followers of Jesus, this book helps us to remember that our purpose in God is continuing to dig into His Word and to live it out daily as it says in Jeremiah 33:3. For those considering who God is, this book will answer many questions and point to the Truth in every way!"   — **Lauri N.**, *Home Educator*

"This book demonstrates exactly how evangelism should be done — with the civility of asking questions! It's amazing how simple questions can become powerful tools that open doors to giving out truth to others. As Mark says, 'People have to think about eternal matters before they can be saved.' How simple it is to ask, 'Why do you believe what you believe?' Asking questions takes all the pressure off of talking to others. I'm hoping my simple questions will become 'pebbles in the shoes' of the people I meet! Read this book! What are you waiting for?"   — **Sally W.,** *Business Owner*

"The most thought-provoking book Mark has written yet! No matter where you are in your journey of faith, be prepared to be challenged. You will be confronted with topics that cannot be ignored and compelled to respond with a sense of urgency to life's most important questions. A must read!"   — **Dave F.,** *Distributor*

"Having come out of the false belief system of Mormonism, I found that few Christians were able to give reasons for their faith. This book exposes the traditions of men and explains the Christian life from the Bible. All Christians, especially our youth before leaving home, need to know what they believe and why they believe it, so they can be effective witnesses for Christ in the world."   — **Kathy S.,** *Christian Educator*

"The emphasis in this book — the questions that Jesus asked — makes this book thought-provoking and challenging. The application is clear, whether responding ourselves to the questions that Jesus asked or utilizing the same technique of asking questions in our witness. Asking questions ought to be a vital part of evangelism, and Mark Cahill has highlighted that very well!"   — **Kristen N.,** *Piano Teacher*

"Insightful and engaging — an excellent study for everyone who loves truth!"   — **Diana B.,** *Computer Testing*

Sincere thanks to:

Jesus Christ

for being the best Question Asker and
the best Question Answerer
of all time.

You have given so many people
throughout the ages
a reason to live and
a reason to die.

Thank you.
See You real soon!

Presented to:

Ten Questions from the King
By Mark Cahill

Third printing, May 2019

ISBN 978-0-9891065-3-5

All Scripture verses cited are from the King James Version.

Editing, Layout, and Cover Design:
    Brenda Nickel

Order additional copies at www.markcahill.org
    or at any bookstore.

Also available in eBook format.

Printed in the United States of America

TABLE OF CONTENTS

Introduction

I love questions! Questions make you think. Good questions can get your synapses firing. Sometimes, a single question can snap you out of life's doldrums and get your mind moving in a whole new direction.

I once saw an article titled: *50 Questions That Will Free Your Mind*. The top ten questions on that list really made my wheels turn:

1. How old would you be if you didn't know how old you were?
2. Which is worse, failing or never trying?
3. If life is so short, why do we do so many things we don't like and like so many things we don't do?
4. When it's all said and done, will you have said more than you've done?
5. What is the one thing you would most like to change about the world?
6. If happiness were the national currency, what kind of work would make you rich?
7. Are you doing what you believe in, or are you settling for what you are doing?
8. If the average human life span were 40 years, how would you live your life differently?
9. To what degree have you actually controlled the course your life has taken?
10. Are you more worried about doing things right, or doing the right things?[1]

The following statement also caught my attention: "Because sometimes asking the right questions is the answer."[2] I've found that, many times, the best thing we can do in a situation is to ask a single, good question. It can get everyone around us thinking. Not all questions need to be answered because, sometimes, the purpose of a good question is to just get us started in processing a new idea.

God has given us the privilege of discovering the answers to the ultimate questions of life.

Questions also help us to arrive at truth. One thing I always tell people is *TETE*: Test Everything and Test Everybody. If we would test whatever people say against the Scriptures, then it would be very, very easy to spot a false teacher. Another thing I say is *QEQE*: Question Everything and Question Everyone. If we wouldn't take *carte blanche* everything that others say as factual, but actually asked questions instead, then we would arrive at truth more quickly and not be fooled into siding with error. Just because someone *says* something or a reporter *reports* something or a crime scene video *shows* something doesn't mean the information is accurate. If you will question everything and question everyone, then you can figure out what is really going on.

Now remember, the point of questioning isn't just to ask questions. That ends up being a waste of valuable time. We need to ask questions to find answers. God has given us the privilege of discovering the answers to the ultimate questions of life, which makes our journey on earth much more exciting.

It is the glory of God to conceal a thing: but the honour of kings *is* to search out a matter. **Proverbs 25:2**

As I was studying the topic of questions, I found some very funny questions out there as well!

- Can you cry under water?
- How important does a person have to be before they are considered assassinated instead of just murdered?

- If money doesn't grow on trees, then why do banks have branches?
- Since bread is square, then why is sandwich meat round?
- Why do you have to "put your two cents in"... but it's only "a penny for your thoughts"? Where's that extra penny going?
- Why does a round pizza come in a square box?
- Why is it that people say they "slept like a baby" when babies wake up like every two hours?
- How come we choose from just two people for President but from fifty for Miss America?
- Why is it that our children can't read a Bible in school but they can in prison?
- Brain cells come and brain cells go, but why do fat cells live forever?
- How can you tell when you run out of invisible ink?
- Did Adam and Eve have navels?
- How does the guy who drives the snowplow get to work in the mornings?
- If a chronic liar tells you he is a chronic liar, do you believe him?
- If all those psychics know the winning lottery numbers, why are they all still working?
- If nothing ever sticks to Teflon, how do they make Teflon stick to the pan?
- If olive oil comes from olives, where does baby oil come from?[3]

Those of you who know me, know that I love a good laugh. Humor, done correctly, is one of God's great gifts to us. But there is a time for humor and a time for seriousness as well. As I was thinking about all of this, I wondered, *What are the best questions that have ever been asked?*

One person put together the following list of his ten greatest philosophical questions of all time:

1. What am I supposed to do?
2. How can we know anything?

3. How do I know what is right or wrong?
4. Who am I?
5. Why all of this stuff and not some other stuff?
6. Why is there something rather than nothing?
7. What happens next?
8. What is the relationship between mind and body?
9. What is the meaning of life?
10. Does God exist?[4]

Many people are asking questions about their existence, and philosophy is not the place they want to turn to for answers. A lady named Cindy contacted the ministry one day. She told me that she had been sitting in a philosophy class at Chapman College one time, when the professor asked this question: "Why do you believe what you believe?" Cindy said this question

"Why do you believe what you believe?"

rocked her world. It hit her like a lightning bolt. She had been raised Christian, but after being asked this question, she really began to consider what it meant to be a Christian. So she pulled out her Bible and started reading and studying, sometimes up to five hours a day. She was shocked to discover how much she didn't know.

Her search for truth prompted her and her family to look for a church that preached about Jesus, although they had a hard time finding one. She was 20 years old when she first heard that question, and now at the age of 68, she has never, ever forgotten that single, profound question! When she saw the "What If?" tract that we offer, she loved all of the questions it poses.

In the Bible, we see a lot of questions being asked, but interestingly, when God asks a question, He already knows the answer. Many lawyers do the same thing in a courtroom to catch someone in a contradiction. Matter of fact, some lawyers are taught to never ask a question in a courtroom

unless they already know the answer! We aren't limited to the standards of an attorney, but we can ask questions of others when we already know the answer, too. We can ask questions to find out more information, to narrow down the discussion a bit, or even to put someone on the spot. Once we have their answers, then we can decide to ask further questions or shift the conversation in a different direction.

I was recently speaking to some college students at Camp Tejas in Texas. I noticed there was a Roman Catholic group there as well. So I walked over to a group of about ten of them, where some were sitting and others were standing around. I greeted them by saying, "Hello." Then I said, "I have a question for you. I want to go to Heaven. What must I do to get there?" Wow! I could tell instantly that this was going to be an intriguing encounter. One of the men, who was dressed like Friar Tuck, spoke only Spanish, so someone translated my question for him. He looked at me and shouted, "Be good!" Then a lady added, "Keep the Ten Commandments!" Her answer provided the perfect opening for me to walk the group through a few of the Ten Commandments. They realized pretty quickly that they had not kept them all. I explained that we are all guilty by the standard of those Ten Commandments and that confession can't help us when we stand before God. We need *forgiveness* of sins, which only Jesus can provide. I will never forget one of the ladies, Kathy, who didn't take her eyes off of me. She soaked up everything I had to say. They all said they liked to read, so I brought them some books at dinner time. All it took was a good question to draw out their opinions about salvation and then compare those beliefs against biblical truth.

We can ask questions to find out more information, to narrow down the discussion a bit, or even to put someone on the spot.

In the LAX Airport one time, I was talking with a Sikh. He told me he has 8.4 million lives to live, and if he gets this life wrong—living as a human—then he has to cycle through 8.4 million lives again! But if he gets this final life in the cycle of progressing through all the different species correct, then he moves on. Typically, Sikhs believe they will blend back into the oneness of god. So I asked him, "Have you gotten this life right?" He looked at me with big eyes and said, "That is a great question!" Seemed simple to me. I imagine I would get a little tired of living after 8.4 million lives! Since I definitely wouldn't want to go through all of those lives again, I would make sure to get this life correct. One simple question really made him think.

"Anyone sensible wants the facts, unless, of course, they have ostrich syndrome!"

On a plane flight to Los Angeles, I was seated across the aisle from a guy who had a big bag filled with a ton of books! So I asked him, "Why do you have so many books?" I had no idea what door that simple question would open! He said he was a college professor. As we continued chatting, it turned out that he was a Religious Studies professor who specialized in Judaism. So I asked him if he was Jewish. He told me that he was an atheist! My wheels started spinning. Then I asked him, "How do you teach the miracles of the Old Testament, like in Exodus?" He said he teaches them from all angles so the students can see them from all sides! Wow! He ended up telling me that he grew up Baptist but teaches at a Methodist college. We had a good, long talk. He eventually said that he considers himself an atheistic Jew. He was very open and said he loves to read, so I gave him a book. I had no clue where that simple question about his books would lead, but I am so glad I asked it!

One of my friends has said, "Well, anyone sensible wants the facts, unless, of course, they have ostrich syndrome!" I like that! So that is what a good question can do; it can take you to the point where you are sharing truth with others.

I pulled up at an intersection to make a left-hand turn one day, and the car next to me, which was stopped at the light, had eight circular Freemasonry emblems on the back of it. Since the driver made the fatal error of having his window rolled down, I asked him through our open windows, "Who is the Great Architect of the Universe?" Some Freemasons call him *GAOTU*. Albert Pike of Freemasonry actually said that Lucifer is the god of Freemasonry. Let's just say that gentleman and I had an amazing conversation right through our open car windows! It was a kind and cordial conversation, and some good seeds were planted to get him thinking.

Either God is going to use you or Satan is going to use you, but you are going to get used. I want to make sure that God is doing the using of my life.

As I was driving out of my parents' neighborhood another day, I noticed a Muslim guy walking toward the mosque down the street. So I stopped, rolled my window down, and chatted with him for a few minutes. I ended up asking him, "Who is Isa? Who is Jesus?" He responded, "A prophet, not the Son of God." I asked him a good, clear question, and he had to give me a clear answer in return. As he walked away at the end of our conversation, he clenched his fist, looked at me, and said, "Mohammad!" That is his choice, even though it is an eternally wrong choice, but I know those questions made him think.

Another thing I always tell people is that either God is going to use you or Satan is going to use you, but you are going to get used. I want to make sure that God is doing the using of my life, and you want the same to be true for you. Asking good questions is a great tool that can allow God to use you mightily to contend for truth with the people you meet.

> Beloved, when I gave all diligence to write unto you of the common salvation, it was needful for me to write unto you, and exhort *you* that ye should earnestly contend for the faith which was once delivered unto the saints. **Jude 1:3**

I started a conversation with three graduate students from Northwestern University while in the O'Hare Airport one time. We continued to talk as we walked toward the plane. Just as we were about to board, the lady in the group who was Russian looked at me and said, "You ask the best questions!" I will never forget my encounter with them, and I am hoping she will never forget the questions that impacted her that day.

What a good question can do is put a pebble in your shoe. Have you ever had grains of sand or a small rock stuck in your shoe? All you can think about is stopping to take off your shoe so you can dump that irritating little piece of creation out of it. That is what a good question can do, too. It makes you stop. It makes you wonder. It rumbles around in your head until you resolve it. This is why it is so important to ask questions and share truth with others as you interact with them.

A good question makes you stop. It makes you wonder. It rumbles around in your head until you resolve it.

Questions are also fun to solve because they make you think. They make you ponder. So where would we find the best questions that have ever been asked? Would we find them in philosophy classes on college campuses? In courtrooms? On the nightly news? Or perhaps in the writings of Solomon, who was the wisest man who ever lived?

> And Solomon's wisdom excelled the wisdom of all the children of the east country, and all the wisdom of Egypt. **1 Kings 4:30**

Even though Solomon was wise, a quick study of his life shows he wasn't perfect.

There has been one, and only one, sinless Person who has ever walked on planet Earth—Jesus Christ. The only Person we should go to for wisdom is the One who has enlightened the minds of men throughout the ages.

And did you know that as Jesus lived His life, He asked many, many questions? In fact, He asked 135 recorded questions in the New Testament! Why would He ask so many questions when He is all-knowing and already knows the answers? I believe the reason He asked questions was, very simply, to make people think—and not only to think, but to draw out their convictions. His questions were direct and put people on the spot. They had to either defend their position or walk away. I also believe He asked questions to bring people face to face with their beliefs, so He could give them truth.

I believe the reason Jesus asked questions was, very simply, to make people think—and not only to think, but to draw out their convictions.

After studying to put this book together, it is rather obvious that Jesus asked the best questions ever. By taking a closer look at some of the Master's fascinating questions, we might learn how to ask good questions as well.

> The entrance of thy words giveth light; it giveth understanding unto the simple. **Psalm 119:130**

> But thou shalt say unto them, This *is* a nation that obeyeth not the voice of the LORD their God, nor receiveth correction: truth is perished, and is cut off from their mouth. **Jeremiah 7:28**

We live in a time where truth seems to have perished from our schools and airwaves. What should Christians be doing about it? Let's learn about some of the questions asked by the King, so we can get more and more people seeking for truth in this lost and dying world.

Introduction
Group Discussion

1. Name some of the reasons why we might ask questions of others. What can questions do for a conversation, and why are they important to ask?

2. Give some examples of questions that you might ask in a conversation. What purpose can various questions serve?

3. What value can rhetorical questions provide in a conversation, and why would we want to ask them?

4. How can a conversation benefit from asking clear and direct questions? What effect can a direct question have in producing a clear response?

5. What do the acronyms TETE and QEQE mean? How can leading someone to test their beliefs against the truth of Scripture help them arrive at the correct answer for salvation?

6. When you have a conversation with a lost person, what clues from your dialogue can prompt you to ask further questions? How might the use of logic and questions work together?

7. Name some of the places in your community where you can find and talk with unsaved people.

8. Now that you know the value of questions, what conversation openers will you use to begin a discussion with a lost person?

9. Come up with two or three excellent questions that would work well to keep conversations going with lost people.

10. What is holding you back from being a person that God can use today to tell someone about the Lord Jesus Christ and the gospel?

Matthew 16:13-16

When Jesus came into the coasts
of Caesarea Philippi,
he asked his disciples, saying,
Whom do men say
that I the Son of man am?

And they said, Some *say that*
thou art John the Baptist:
some, Elias; and others, Jeremias,
or one of the prophets.

He saith unto them,
But whom say ye that I am?

And Simon Peter answered and said,
Thou art the Christ,
the Son of the living God.

CHAPTER 1

Do You Have Major League Faith?

OPINIONS

Caesarea Philippi is the northernmost point in Israel that Jesus reached during His ministry. It was the apex, so to speak. Seems like a perfect place to ask the ultimate question: *Whom do men say that I am?*

Jesus knows He is the talk of the town. He knows people have opinions about Him. He also knows the disciples have been talking to them. So when Jesus asks His disciples, "Whom do men say that I am?" He wants to know from them what the people of Israel are saying about Him.

Everyone has opinions. They not only like to share them, but we like to hear them, too. We want to know what they think about their favorite sports team, food, vacation spot, or even their attitudes about their boss! Opinions are fascinating because they tell us a lot about someone's preferences and beliefs.

We also want to know what people are saying about Jesus. What are they saying around the water cooler? What are they saying on Television, Twitter, and Facebook about Him? Even as people waste time on all of those gadgets and apps, they are still making comments about Him and His identity, and we want to know what they are saying.

So if you want to learn about someone's viewpoints, just ask them. Pretty simple. Most people like to chat and give their opinions, so ask them the question: *Who do you think Jesus is?* You will get all kinds of answers, and I guarantee it will spice up a conversation rather quickly!

Famous people throughout history have also had a variety of interesting opinions about Jesus as well:

"Alexander, Caesar, Charlemagne, and myself founded empires; but what foundation did we rest the creations of our genius? Upon force. Jesus Christ founded an empire upon love; and at this hour millions of men would die for Him."
—Napoleon Bonaparte[5]

"A man who was completely innocent, offered himself as a sacrifice for the good of others, including his enemies, and became the ransom of the world. It was a perfect act."
—Mahatma Gandhi[6]

"Christianity will go. It will vanish and shrink. I needn't argue with that; I'm right and I will be proved right. We're more popular than Jesus now; I don't know which will go first—rock and roll or Christianity."
—John Lennon[7]

"The day will come when the mystical generation of Jesus by the Supreme Being in the womb of a virgin, will be classed with the fable of the generation of Minerva in the brain of Jupiter."
—Thomas Jefferson[8]

"I am an historian, I am not a believer, but I must confess as a historian that this penniless preacher from Nazareth is irrevocably the very center of history. Jesus Christ is easily the most dominant figure in all history."
—H. G. Wells[9]

CHAPTER 1

"Despite our efforts to keep him out, God intrudes. The life of Jesus is bracketed by two impossibilities: a virgin's womb and an empty tomb. Jesus entered our world through a door marked, 'No Entrance' and left through a door marked 'No Exit.'"
—Peter Larson[10]

"I think Jesus was a compassionate, super-intelligent gay man who understood human problems. On the cross, he forgave the people who crucified him. Jesus wanted us to be loving and forgiving. I don't know what makes people so cruel. Try being a gay woman in the Middle East—you're as good as dead."
—Elton John[11]

"As to Jesus of Nazareth, my opinion of whom you particularly desire, I think the system of morals and his religion, as he left them to us, is the best the world ever saw, or is likely to see; But I apprehend it has received various corrupting changes, and I have, with most of the present dissenters in England, some doubts as to his divinity..."
—Benjamin Franklin[12]

"As a child, I received instruction both in the Bible and in the Talmud. I am a Jew, but I am enthralled by the luminous figure of the Nazarene.... No one can read the Gospels without feeling the actual presence of Jesus. His personality pulsates in every word. No myth is filled with such life."
—Albert Einstein[13]

"I would like to ask Him if He was indeed virgin born, because the answer to that question would define history."
—Larry King[14]

EVERYDAY PEOPLE

Notice that Jesus is not asking His disciples what the religious folks are saying. He already knows what the Scribes and Pharisees think of Him. He is asking what the regular person thinks. He wants to know who the common folks say that He is. Too many times, we turn to religious figures

23

on television and parrot what they say. Or we listen to some professor in college who spends an entire semester ripping apart the Bible. Jesus knows these people exist, but He wants to know what the regular folks think about Him. There is just something about the simplicity of common folks and their

opinions that Jesus wants to hear, but I want to hear the opinions of everyday people, too. I enjoy a good conversation with a regular person more than with a highfalutin person any day of the week.

One thing I tell people is the world has questions and Christians have answers.

Jesus' question also implies that the disciples were talking with and asking questions of the people, too. So ask yourself: Do you live your life this way? Do you hang out with others? Do you ask them questions? Do you answer their questions? One thing I tell people is the world has questions and Christians have answers. But we have got to go and meet with these people who have questions. Every now and then, they wind up on our doorsteps, but most of the time, we have to cross the threshold of our front doors and go out into the world to find them. Since Jesus was a man of the people and the disciples were, too, then we need to be men and women of the people as well.

The people in Jesus' day probably had questions about whether He would call everyone to repentance, like John the Baptist. Would He keep doing miracles, like Elijah? Would He keep speaking the words of God, like Jeremiah and the other prophets? They were trying to figure Him out, which is always a good thing.

When Jesus asks about the opinions of the people, He also knows their viewpoints might carry the undertones of either honoring and respecting Him or perhaps dishonoring Him as well. The people really did not know Who was standing before them. Jesus was trying to open their eyes to see who He was because if they realized that He was the fulfillment of their Scriptures, they could become His true and faithful followers all the way to the end.

GOING PUBLIC

Jesus not only wants to know who the people say He is, but He wants to know who His disciples say He is, too. He is not ignorant of their beliefs, but He wants them to make a declarative statement. He wants them to publicly say what they believe. He wants it on the record! This is very important. We all have opinions, thoughts, and ideas, but we can keep those viewpoints hidden and locked away from public view. There are certain things that should never remain hidden. We should always proclaim the love we have for our spouse publicly. There is nothing wrong with bragging about your kids. They are your kids! We should also never, ever keep our spiritual beliefs hidden either. They should be open and public for everyone to see.

Stating something publicly has the effect of actually strengthening what you believe.

Whenever a supposedly famous person dies, many times I will google their name to find out about their spiritual beliefs. Then I look at their life to see if it lined up with their profession of faith. The late rock star Prince was raised Seventh Day Adventist but later became a devout Jehovah's Witness. At one point in his career, he purportedly said, "Everything is about Jesus and the Bible." What a fascinating statement, but did he actually live that way? Did his recorded music and concerts drive people to find out about the Creator of the universe?

Another interesting aspect of stating something publicly is its effect of actually strengthening what you believe. It causes your faith to grow stronger. Why? You have declared it. People know where you stand, and now you have to back it up with your life! Again, this is one reason why people stay silent on many major topics. They know that when they say something publicly, they have to live it publicly as well. But, of course, that is what Jesus wants us to do. He wants us to never be ashamed of Him, either in our words or in our actions.

SIDING WITH TRUTH

Jesus also asks His disciples, "Whom say ye that I am?" to find out which side of the fence they are on. This question is one that everyone will have to answer at some point in their existence, either here or on the other side. There is no avoiding this one, and the disciples couldn't avoid it either.

> Suppose ye that I am come to give peace on earth? I tell you, Nay; but rather division:
>
> **Luke 12:51**

The true Christ will always cause division because people must decide which side of the fence they are on.

Remember that Jesus Christ brings division. He knows that not everyone likes Him. Not everyone wants to come to Him, obey Him, or surrender to Him. The true Christ will always cause division because people must decide which side of the fence they are on.

So when Jesus asks this question of His disciples, it becomes much more personal. No hiding out or sitting on the sidelines. Jesus asks a question and wants an answer. It's *put-up or shut-up* time, as they say.

Keep in mind that the disciples had an intimate relationship with Jesus. They were with Him day in and day out. They hung out with Him and watched Him up close. Would their answers be the same as the people who observed Him from a distance? Had their closeness to Him led them to a different conclusion?

How about you? Has your knowledge of the Lord become more intimate through the years, or have you been sidelined in your walk of faith? Are you hiding your Christian walk from others, or are you living a bold and public life of faith in Jesus Christ?

THE SPOKESMAN

Jesus asks this question of the group, but it is Peter who responds. There is a time to stand up and speak up. There is a time to let your beliefs be heard and to not blend in with the shadows. Are you standing up in those moments, or are you shrinking back from your duty to confess Christ?

> Go, stand and speak in the temple to the people all the words of this life. **Acts 5:20**

When Peter came out in the open and publicly declared that Jesus is the Christ, he was pointing out the divinity of Jesus. Jesus is God incarnate. He is God who has taken on human flesh. This is a huge point. Satan gives us a lot of false messiahs out there, but you need the real One, who, of course, is God in the flesh.

There is a time to stand up and speak up. There is a time to let your beliefs be heard and to not blend in with the shadows.

> And without controversy great is the mystery of godliness: God was manifest in the flesh, justified in the Spirit, seen of angels, preached unto the Gentiles, believed on in the world, received up into glory. **1 Timothy 3:16**

I was once voted to be the foreman of a jury, and when it came time to present the verdict, I knew I was speaking for the group. Before leaving the jury room, I asked each juror if they could affirm to the judge that the defendant was guilty, if they were asked to stand up and do so. I wanted to make sure everyone was convinced of the verdict. So when we all walked into the courtroom, I had no problem giving that verdict to the judge because I knew I was backed up by eleven other people.

This makes me wonder about the disciples. What questions about Jesus did they sit around and talk about? Those had to be some fun times and some amazing discussions! But I am sure that at some point they discussed: *Hey fellas, be honest with me now. Who do you REALLY think He is?*

So when the day came and they got that question from the King, Peter was ready. I wonder if the group was thinking, *I am sure glad Peter answered that question and not me!* It makes me wonder how many of the disciples were ready to answer in the same way.

Your feet are making steps today. You are either walking toward the cross or away from it.

Can you imagine the Son of God looking directly at you with fire in His eyes and asking you that question? No worries, your day will come, and you must have the right answer on that day.

STAND OR WALK AWAY

Walking away from Jesus is always a possibility. Your feet are making steps today. You are either walking toward the cross or away from it. There is no neutral ground with the King.

> From that *time* many of his disciples went back, and walked no more with him.   **John 6:66**

People walk away from Jesus today, and they walked away from Jesus back then. Why did they do that after hearing His teachings and seeing Him perform miracles? Did they really not understand who He was? Did they not want the persecution that comes with following Him? Did they not want to abandon all for Him? I have actually had atheists tell me that even though they had no evidence that God didn't exist, they knew they would no longer be in control of their lives if they admitted that He did exist. But if those in Jesus' day really knew who He was, and if they deep down knew He was the Son of God, how could they walk away? In actuality, they couldn't. Jesus was pressing them on this point. They needed to make a proclamation and stick with what they knew to be true.

This is why the question, *Who is Jesus?* is good to ask. It makes people's feet move. They will either move closer to the cross or farther away. It won't let them sit in the mushy middle. Once, I asked this question of an atheist, and the question really made him squirm. He responded, "Well, he is not some blond-haired, blue-eyed guy from the Middle East!" He really didn't answer my question, but I didn't let him off the hook. I kept pressing for an answer, and we ended up having a nice give and take.

You belong on the Major League Faith team and that team alone. You know who Jesus is, so make your stand and never turn back.

> *Which* when Jesus perceived, he said unto them, O ye of little faith, why reason ye among yourselves, because ye have brought no bread?
> **Matthew 16:8**

You see, Jesus did not want His followers to fall into the group of those who had little faith. That is a team you do not want to join. You weren't designed for the Little League Faith team. You have trained too hard, studied too much, and sought to obey the Lord too often. Instead, you belong on the Major League Faith team and that team alone. You know who Jesus is, so make your stand and never turn back.

ETERNITY IS COMING

At the end of the day, it doesn't matter who your parents think Jesus is. It doesn't matter who your grandmama or your grandpapa thinks He is. It really doesn't matter what your roommate thinks of Him either. What matters is who do *you* think He is? Why? Because you will die. You will stand before the King, and that is not the day to have the wrong answer. It is okay to have the wrong answer on a calculus test, but you must not have the wrong answer on the day you have your one-on-one meeting with the Master of the Universe.

What matters is who do you think Jesus is? Why? Because you will die. You will stand before the King. And that is not the day to have the wrong answer.

The good news is that He doesn't want you to have the wrong answer on that day either! He wants you to be right with Him and to serve Him boldly all of the days of your life!

But remember, Jesus also asked this question because He knew Calvary was coming. He needed to know their answer because He didn't want them walking away from Him after His crucifixion.

This ultimate question is one we don't want to run away from either. It is a question we want to ask people. I was talking to a student at Cal State Fullerton one time. We were having a good conversation about spiritual matters. Then I asked him, "Who do you think Jesus is?" He said, "Hey man, I don't want to go there." He was trying to get far, far away from that question! It was sad but funny at the same time. I have had people tell me that Jesus was a good man, a great teacher, and that He existed and died on the cross, but He didn't rise from the dead. How people answer this question will reverberate throughout eternity, which means it is a question that is way too important to avoid with friends and strangers.

After chatting with that student, I wound up talking with another student who had a big Jewish flag on her shirt. I asked Chandler (pronounced chandelier), "Are you Jewish, or are you a Christian who supports Israel?" She let me know she was Jewish. I then asked her if she ever catches flak for her shirt. In case you don't know, there is a lot of anti-Semitism taking place on college campuses right now. It is hidden under the guise of the BDS movement, which stands for Boycott, Divestment, and Sanctions against Israel. She told me she was tossed out of a Palestinian restaurant in Los Angeles one time because they didn't like her shirt! I just love it when so-called tolerant people show their true colors. She then looked at me and said, "Can I ask you a question?" I responded, "Sure." She asked, "Jesus: Was He just a man, was He a prophet, or was He God?"! That is like the dream question you always want someone to ask! So keep in mind, not only did Jesus ask this question, but people might actually ask you this question one day as well.

WHO DO YOU SAY THAT I AM?

Jesus is the Christ! He is the Anointed One. He is, at long last, the Messiah the Jews had been waiting for. Do not put Him in the low category of being merely a good guy, a rabbi, a good son to His parents, or any other category where He doesn't belong. Keep Him in His rightful position, and live your life accordingly.

In our chapter's main passage, the statement "Thou art the Christ, the Son of the living God" is included. The word *living* is very important because Jesus is the living Savior. Zoroaster, Krishna, Buddha, Confucius, Mohammed, Joseph Smith, and Mary Baker Eddy are all dead. Jesus is alive and well because He is the living God! The tombs of all other religious figures are full of bones, but the Lord's tomb is empty. His resurrection is a key point to both remember and share

Jesus is alive and well because He is the living God! The tombs of all other religious figures are full of bones, but the Lord's tomb is empty.

because it sets Him apart from every other religious leader in the history of the world.

And if Christ be not risen, then *is* our preaching vain, and your faith *is* also vain.

1 Corinthians 15:14

Always remember that your truthful confession for Christ matters.

Always remember that your truthful confession for Christ matters. Consider the public testimonies of these early believers, and see if your public testimony is the same.

What did the apostle Peter confess?

Then Simon Peter answered him, Lord, to whom shall we go? thou hast the words of eternal life. And we believe and are sure that thou art that Christ, the Son of the living God.   **John 6:68,69**

What did Martha believe?

She saith unto him, Yea, Lord: I believe that thou art the Christ, the Son of God, which should come into the world.   **John 11:27**

What did the Ethiopian eunuch proclaim?

And Philip said, If thou believest with all thine heart, thou mayest. And he answered and said, I believe that Jesus Christ is the Son of God.   **Acts 8:37**

What did the apostle Paul preach?

And straightway he preached Christ in the synagogues, that he is the Son of God.   **Acts 9:20**

What did the apostle John exhort?

Whosoever shall confess that Jesus is the Son of God, God dwelleth in him, and he in God.   **1 John 4:15**

Whosoever believeth that Jesus is the Christ is born of God: and every one that loveth him that begat loveth him also that is begotten of him.

1 John 5:1

And many other signs truly did Jesus in the presence of his disciples, which are not written in this book: But these are written, that ye might believe that Jesus is the Christ, the Son of God; and that believing ye might have life through his name.

John 20:30,31

What did the apostle Thomas declare?

And Thomas answered and said unto him, My Lord and my God.

John 20:28

Incidentally, how did Jesus respond to the kind of faith that openly confesses Him?

Jesus saith unto him, Thomas, because thou hast seen me, thou hast believed: blessed *are* they that have not seen, and *yet* have believed. **John 20:29**

Make sure you can stand boldly and without shame before the Lord Jesus Christ, knowing that you have given Him your best by openly declaring Him to the world!

But Jesus warned:

Jesus answered and said unto them, Ye do err, not knowing the scriptures, nor the power of God. **Matthew 22:29**

Do not err by not knowing the Scriptures that tell us about the Lord Jesus Christ. By the way, who do you say that He is? And by the way, who are you going to be asking that question of today? And lastly, who will you be sharing the right answer to that question with today as well? Make sure you can stand boldly and without shame before the Lord Jesus Christ, knowing that you have given Him your best by openly declaring Him to the world!

Chapter 1
Group Discussion

1. When you talk to people, what opinions and viewpoints of theirs do you most want to know? How can you bring their opinions about Jesus Christ to the surface?

2. Think about the people you spend time with and their opinions of Jesus. In your circle of friends, who should be influencing whom and why? How are you preparing others with the right answers for Judgment Day?

3. What questions can you ask people that will reveal their opinions about the Bible, Jesus Christ, and salvation? Why is discussing these subjects important? How can these questions affect someone's life today and in eternity?

4. Judging from the various media, academic, religious, and entertainment sources around us, what would you say are the most common views of Jesus Christ held by people today? Name some of the influences that have shaped those views.

5. Knowing that opinions about Jesus differ significantly, what qualifies someone to speak accurately about the Bible, Jesus Christ, and the gospel? Whom should we allow to teach us about eternal truth?

6. Give an example of someone you know who has turned away from the facts about Jesus because they listened to the opinions of so-called "experts." What steps have you taken to correct that misinformation, and what has been the outcome so far?

7. If your friends, family, or co-workers were to stand trial before the Lord today, what eternal verdict would be rendered for them? If that courtroom scene has you concerned, what steps can you take today to overturn the evidence that is mounting against them?

8. Have you gone public or have you been private about your faith in Jesus Christ? Give reasons for your answer, and what you would like to change.

9. Name a time when you were given an opportunity to openly declare Jesus Christ to others. What were the circumstances? What opposition did you face? Why were you glad for making that stand? What regrets would you have today if you had remained silent?

10. Are you ready for the day that you will stand before the Lord? What answer will you have for the question, *Whom say ye that I am?* What changes do you need to make in your life to prepare yourself for that day?

Matthew 21:42-46

Jesus saith unto them,
Did ye never read in the scriptures,
The stone which the builders rejected,
the same is become the head of the corner:
this is the Lord's doing,
and it is marvellous in our eyes?

Therefore say I unto you,
The kingdom of God shall be taken from you,
and given to a nation bringing
forth the fruits thereof.

And whosoever shall fall on this stone
shall be broken:
but on whomsoever it shall fall,
it will grind him to powder.

And when the chief priests and Pharisees
had heard his parables,
they perceived that he spake of them.

But when they sought to lay hands on him,
they feared the multitude,
because they took him for a prophet.

CHAPTER 2

Is Jesus Your Cornerstone or Stumbling Stone?

THE SCRIPTURES

One error you never want to make as you follow the Lord is to not trust His Book. The Bible either contains the words of eternal life, or it does not. We either live by this Book, or we need to put it back on the shelf. And by the way, it belongs on the top shelf with no other book anywhere near it!

So if someone asked you if they could trust the Word of God, how would you answer them? The Bible actually provides the certainty that both you and they need.

Consider how God can authenticate His Book when there is no one greater than Himself to validate its message. What factual evidence can He provide that will persuade you and others that the Bible is true? A friend of mine uses the following example to convince the lost about the reliability of the Bible:

Imagine you were the most important person who has ever walked the face of the earth (which you are not), and let's say it's critically important that humanity knows who you are for a

variety of reasons. Let's say God inspires forty people over 1,500 years on three continents in three languages to write about you so that people will recognize you when the time comes. And let's say all that information about you is recorded in a book. When you finally arrive on the scene and fulfill the prophecies written about you, three things happen at once: It validates you because what was written about you is true, it validates God for knowing the details about your life ahead of time, and it validates the body of writing it was recorded in. This is what God did to validate Jesus, Himself, and the Bible, all at the same time.

Of course, this example illustrates how the truth about Jesus, God, and the Bible can be trusted, and it all hinges on fulfilled prophecy. Let's put that into perspective for you.

Did you know that the chances of being struck by lightning are one in 100,000? "Mega Millions and Powerball websites list your chances of winning their jackpots at about one in 200 million, or $1 \times 10(8)$."[15]

Now let's take a look at the probability of just 40 of the prophecies about the Messiah coming true. What would be the odds of that happening?

> "The combined probability of all these forty events happening is one times ten to the 136th power $\{10(136)\}$. That is a 1 with 136 zeros! You might want to get out a piece of paper and try to write a 1 with 136 zeros on it, just to get an idea of how large that number really is."
> —Stephen Bauer[16]

Did you know that "a normal pinhead can hold around 5 billion atoms?"[17] A drop of water contains around 100 billion atoms, or $1 \times 10(11)$. The entire earth contains about $1 \times 10(50)$ atoms.

> "Estimates are that the observable universe, including all planets, 21 moons, and stars in the entire sky, contains approximately $1 \times 10(81)$ atoms."
> —Stephen Bauer[18]

That is an incredibly large number, but yet, it's not even close to the odds of just 40 prophecies coming true for the Messiah.

Dr. Emile Borel, who is one of the foremost experts on mathematical probability, says this about the likelihood of events occurring in our world:

> "The basic law of probability states that the occurrence of any event in which the chances are beyond 10(50) or one in one followed by fifty zeros (10 to the 50th power), is an event that we can state with certainty will never happen, no matter how many conceivable opportunities could exist for the event to take place."
>
> **—Dr. Emile Borel**[19]

As you can see, it is a mathematical impossibility for these prophecies to come true in anyone, yet they all came true in Jesus Christ! As a matter of fact, more than 300 of them came true in His life! This is probably the biggest piece of evidence that the Bible is true and that Jesus is the Messiah who is spoken of in the Old Testament. It is irrefutable that He fulfilled all of these prophecies.

So when God says His Word is true, it is absolutely true. The staggering improbability of over 300 prophecies being fulfilled in the first coming of Jesus Christ suggests that what we know about God,

You can throw the full weight of your faith on every word of God found in the Bible.

Jesus, and the Bible are the most certain facts known to man. And that means you can throw the full weight of your faith on every word of God found in the Bible.

> Thy word *is* true *from* the beginning: and every one of thy righteous judgments *endureth* for ever. **Psalm 119:160**

> Every word of God *is* pure: he *is* a shield unto them that put their trust in him. **Proverbs 30:5**

And the Word was made flesh, and dwelt among us, (and we beheld his glory, the glory as of the only begotten of the Father,) full of grace and truth. **John 1:14**

CORNERSTONES

The Scriptures talk a lot about the "head of the corner" or the "chief cornerstone." God uses the illustration of cornerstones to draw our attention to the Cornerstone He has chosen to build His house.

Therefore thus saith the Lord GOD, Behold, I lay in Zion for a foundation a stone, a tried stone, a precious corner *stone,* a sure foundation: he that believeth shall not make haste. **Isaiah 28:16**

Typically, a cornerstone is the first stone to be set in place whenever a structure is built, and all other stones in the building are aligned to it. Cornerstones mark the beginning point of construction, unite walls at intersections, and determine the positioning of the building. They support and set the reference point for how an entire framework comes together.

Cornerstones often represent "the nominal starting place in the construction of a monumental building, usually carved with the date and laid in place with appropriate ceremonies."[20] You may have seen the famous picture of George Washington laying the cornerstone of the U.S. Capitol building. These stones can be symbolic or ceremonial in nature, and many times, they are inscribed with information about the building's importance and why it was built.

Be it known unto you all, and to all the people of Israel, that by the name of Jesus Christ of Nazareth, whom ye crucified, whom God raised from the dead, *even* by him doth this man stand here before you whole. This is the stone which was set at nought of you builders, which is become the head of the corner. Neither is there salvation in any other: for there is none other name under heaven given among men, whereby we must be saved. **Acts 4:10-12**

Now therefore ye are no more strangers and foreigners, but fellowcitizens with the saints, and of the household of God; And are built upon the foundation of the apostles and prophets, Jesus Christ himself being the chief corner *stone;* In whom all the building fitly framed together groweth unto an holy temple in the Lord: **Ephesians 2:19-21**

Generally, the term *cornerstone* is used in Scripture to illustrate the foundational importance of Jesus for the entire building of God's house. He is the cornerstone that joins the whole structure of the household of God together. Putting a building together requires the right foundation, and the cornerstone makes the entire structure complete. Likewise, Jesus is the cornerstone of your faith and the One who can finish your life completely.

REJECTED

When building a structure, builders and masons inspect and test stones to see if they are fit to be used as cornerstones. If they are unsuitable for the job, they are cast aside and called *rejected,* which is an "expression borrowed from masons, who, finding a stone, which being tried in a particular place, and appearing improper for it, is thrown aside, and another taken; however, at last, it may happen that the very stone which had been before rejected, may be found the most suitable as the head stone of the corner."[21] The builder may realize later that one of the rocks he cast aside earlier is actually perfect for being used as the cornerstone.

Jesus is the cornerstone that joins the whole structure of the household of God together.

This seems to be spiritually true as well. Many Jews have set Jesus aside because He is not the Messiah they were expecting. When witnessing to Jews, I use the following verses to show them that Jesus is indeed their

Messiah: Isaiah 53, Psalm 22, Daniel 9:24-27, Jeremiah 31:31-34, and Proverbs 30:4. Often, they—like the Jews in Jesus' day—reject the evidence that is found in their own Scriptures.

To whom coming, *as unto* a living stone, disallowed indeed of men, but chosen of God, *and* precious, Ye also, as lively stones, are built up a spiritual house, an holy priesthood, to offer up spiritual sacrifices, acceptable to God by Jesus Christ. Wherefore also it is contained in the scripture, Behold, I lay in Sion a chief corner stone, elect, precious: and he that believeth on him shall not be confounded. Unto you therefore which believe *he is* precious: but unto them which be disobedient, the stone which the builders disallowed, the same is made the head of the corner, And a stone of stumbling, and a rock of offence, *even to them* which stumble at the word, being disobedient: whereunto also they were appointed. **1 Peter 2:4-8**

So don't miss this: Jesus is the foundation upon which salvation rests.

The stone *which* the builders refused is become the head *stone* of the corner. This is the LORD's doing; it *is* marvellous in our eyes.
Psalm 118:22,23

Jesus may be rejected by the Jews, but He is a perfect fit for the cross! So don't miss this: Jesus is the foundation upon which salvation rests. He is the Cornerstone that can unite Jews and Gentiles together in the household of God, if the Jews will accept Him as their Messiah.

STUMBLING OVER THE STONE

Keep in mind that in our passage, Jesus was speaking to the theologians of the day. Any leader who represents God needs to uphold truth, yet we see Jesus challenging the authority of the Scribes and Pharisees over their ignorance of the Word. Reading the Scriptures is one thing, but understanding them is another story altogether. Teachers are not infallible, which is why you need to spend time studying the Scriptures for yourself.

> And he shall be for a sanctuary; but for a stone of stumbling and for a rock of offence to both the houses of Israel, for a gin and for a snare to the inhabitants of Jerusalem. And many among them shall stumble, and fall, and be broken, and be snared, and be taken.
> **Isaiah 8:14,15**

The chief priests and elders realized that Jesus spoke of them as the ones who would stumble. Truth was piercing their hearts, their souls, and their guilty consciences, and they were getting angry. The rock of offense had put a clear choice before them. Either trip over this Stone and fall flat on their faces, or fall flat on their faces in repentance and believe on Him. What choice would they make: repentance or revenge?

Teachers are not infallible, which is why you need to spend time studying the Scriptures for yourself.

These leaders of Israel should have been building up the household of God, but they were building their own "building," so to speak, and they wouldn't let the chief Cornerstone into their house! They tried to make Jesus a stepping stone to be trampled upon by others in order to keep their own building intact.

> But Israel, which followed after the law of righteousness, hath not attained to the law of righteousness. Wherefore? Because *they sought it* not by faith, but as it were by the works of the law. For they stumbled at that stumblingstone; As it is written, Behold, I lay in Sion a stumblingstone and rock of offence: and whosoever believeth on him shall not be ashamed.
> **Romans 9:31-33**

The Jews tried, as many people do today, to attain the kingdom of God by works. Salvation has not worked that way in previous millennia, and it won't work that way now. We are justified by faith, and faith alone, and not by works lest anyone should boast about those works for all of eternity. Instead, we need to be boasting about what Jesus did for us on the cross for all of eternity!

> Where *is* boasting then? It is excluded. By what law? of works? Nay: but by the law of faith. Therefore we conclude that a man is justified by faith without the deeds of the law.　**Romans 3:27,28**

> Therefore being justified by faith, we have peace with God through our Lord Jesus Christ:　**Romans 5:1**

> For by grace are ye saved through faith; and that not of yourselves: *it is* the gift of God: Not of works, lest any man should boast. For we are his workmanship, created in Christ Jesus unto good works, which God hath before ordained that we should walk in them.
> **Ephesians 2:8-10**

Many times, I ask people, "When you die, what do you think is out there? What do you think happens when you die?"

Many times, I ask people, "When you die, what do you think is out there? What do you think happens when you die?" They often tell me they believe there is a heaven. Then I ask, "Do you think there is a hell, too?" Most everyone says *yes*.

Typically, I turn it around on them and say, "I want to go to Heaven. What do I have to do to get there?" You see, that puts them on the spot. Now they have to come up with an answer to that question. As we said in the last chapter, questions are a good way to get people to think. Usually, they give me one of two responses: Either *be a good person* to go there, or *believe in the Lord Jesus Christ for the forgiveness of my sins.* I get those answers all the time, but the Cornerstone knows that only one of those answers is correct. The Cornerstone will either bring life to you for believing, or the Cornerstone will crush you for trying to come to Him through works.

When Jesus announced that the kingdom would be "taken from you," He was letting the Jews know there would be consequences for their actions and unbelief. While the Jews have largely seen Jesus as a rock of offense, Scripture tells us they have stumbled, but not so as to fall. They have been broken by the Rock and dispersed throughout the world, but when Jesus returns in the end of days, all Israel will be saved.

> I say then, Have they stumbled that they should fall? God forbid: but *rather* through their fall salvation *is come* unto the Gentiles, for to provoke them to jealousy....And they also, if they abide not still in unbelief, shall be grafted in: for God is able to graft them in again....And so all Israel shall be saved:...   **Romans 11:11,23,26**

Those who *fell* were disappointed in Messiah. They despised that He came in lowliness and died on a cross with thieves. The Jews expected a warrior King who would fight for Israel instead. Their unrealistic expectations let them down because they were not grounded in truth.

Just think about the eternal ramifications for not understanding the Scriptures. These leaders handled the Word constantly, yet they missed the prophecies concerning the Messiah and didn't recognize Him when He was standing in front of them. Everyone could walk up to this *building* of Jesus and see how beautiful it was in all its perfection. Yet, they rejected Him, and soon, they would want Him dead.

Just think about the eternal ramifications for not understanding the Scriptures.

Instead of repenting, the Pharisees seethed with anger toward the One who had exposed their hearts. The One telling them the truth had become their bitter enemy. Even though they schemed to put Jesus to death, a death sentence now awaited them. They would be crushed by the Stone they rejected.

STONING

Stoning was a form of capital punishment used in the Old Testament as a way to execute both people and animals. There were certain sins that required this judgment. This punishment was only meted out after a guilty verdict was given in a trial with at least two witnesses who testified against the accused. The Jews needed to make sure they did not make any mistakes by condemning an innocent man. The witnesses against the accused were the ones to cast the first stones. One instance of *illegal* stoning recorded in the Bible occurred with Stephen and can be found at the end of chapter 7 in the book of Acts.

When the hammer of judgment falls, the condemned will be completely destroyed without a trace. They will be ground to powder, and like chaff on a threshing floor, they will be winnowed away forever.

"The place of stoning was twice as high as a man; while standing on this, one of the witnesses struck the culprit on the loins, so that he fell over this scaffold; if he died by the stroke and fall, well; if not, the other witness threw a stone upon his heart, and dispatched him. That stone thrown on the culprit was, in some cases, as much as two men could lift up."[22]

Stoning carries the idea of destruction, shattering, and pulverizing to dust. When the hammer of judgment falls, the condemned will be completely destroyed without a trace. They will be ground to powder, and like chaff on a threshing floor, they will be winnowed away forever.

CRUSHED BY THE STONE

Jesus was actually offering the Kingdom to Israel, but they stumbled at the thought of accepting Him as King. So their house would be left desolate and taken from them. The King was turning toward those who loved Him and who would produce the fruits worthy of His Kingdom.

In the book of Daniel, we learn that in the end of days, the Stone that is cut without hands will strike and topple the kingdoms of the earth and break them to pieces so that they blow away like chaff on a threshing floor. Then the Stone will grow to become an enduring kingdom that will never end. Are you part of that enduring kingdom? Or are you giving your strength toward building the kingdoms that will be gone with the wind?

In the end of days, the Stone that is cut without hands will strike and topple the kingdoms of the earth and break them to pieces so that they blow away like chaff on a threshing floor.

Thou sawest till that a stone was cut out without hands, which smote the image upon his feet *that were* of iron and clay, and brake them to pieces. Then was the iron, the clay, the brass, the silver, and the gold, broken to pieces together, and became like the chaff of the summer threshingfloors; and the wind carried them away, that no place was found for them: and the stone that smote the image became a great mountain, and filled the whole earth. . . . And in the days of these kings shall the God of heaven set up a kingdom, which shall never be destroyed: and the kingdom shall not be left to other people, *but* it shall break in pieces and consume all these kingdoms, and it shall stand for ever.

Daniel 2:34,35,44

The Stone will crush everything that gets in its way. Either fall on the Rock for mercy and forgiveness, or the Stone will break you in pieces. There is no getting around that Jesus will win in the end. The question is whether or not He is winning in your life today.

FALSE FOUNDATIONS

Throughout history, many have stumbled over God and His truth. Rather than seeking to be part of God's kingdom, they have sought to build their own kingdoms instead. Just like Balak, the ancient King of Moab, these leaders put stumbling blocks before the children of God to entice them to eat foods sacrificed to idols and to worship other gods. Beware of false teachers who entice you to enter into their counterfeit religious systems, which lead not only to worshiping false images of God but also to being crushed by the Cornerstone in the end.

Just remember that if the correct Cornerstone is not properly set as the foundation of your life or church, there will be major problems in the long run.

But I have a few things against thee, because thou hast there them that hold the doctrine of Balaam, who taught Balac to cast a stumblingblock before the children of Israel, to eat things sacrificed unto idols, and to commit fornication. **Revelation 2:14**

And he brought him to Jesus. And when Jesus beheld him, he said, Thou art Simon the son of Jona: thou shalt be called Cephas, which is by interpretation, A stone. **John 1:42**

Speaking of stones, the Roman Catholic church teaches that Peter was the rock upon which their church was built. No, Peter was just a living stone used as a brick in the building of God. Please keep in mind that a false view of the real Cornerstone can have eternal consequences. Jesus is the true Rock, and Peter is a small stone. Just remember that if the correct Cornerstone is not properly set as the foundation of your life or church, there will be major problems in the long run. The proper placement of Christ in your life will keep things theologically sound and protect you from falling into false teachings.

The Bible takes a stand on every major issue we deal with today from abortion, gay marriage, self-defense, alcohol, sex, private property to pretty much any other concern of our time. When talking with my mom the other day, our conversation veered into how wicked the world has become since the time she was young. I told her that we can basically look at any position the Bible takes on a particular topic, and the world will say that the opposite position is okay. It really got her thinking. That is the culture we live in today. But it implores us to know our Bibles so that we can stand against the untruths found in media, classrooms, politics, and false religions, which cause people to stumble and trip today.

The ways of the world or the ways of the King — which one will you choose?

"It is impossible to mentally or socially enslave
a Bible-reading people."
—Horace Greeley[23]

"I have known ninety-five of the world's great men in my time,
and of these, eighty-seven were followers of the Bible."
—William Gladstone[24]

"The Bible is the rock on which our republic rests."
—Andrew Jackson[25]

These men knew the importance of God's Word. Can you say the same?

So what is the foundation of your life? Is the chief Cornerstone your true foundation, and is He crushing everything that is unbiblical in your life today, or will He crush you one day? If you have the Word of God and Jesus as your chief Cornerstone, don't be surprised if God uses you in a mighty way for Him in the days to come! The ways of the world or the ways of the King—which one will you choose?

Chapter 2
Group Discussion

1. Give a few details about how and when the Cornerstone of Jesus Christ was laid in your life. Did good works play any part in your salvation? Why or why not?

2. Give examples of how abiding in God's Word blesses you and others around you. How does dwelling in truth help you to reach the lost?

3. Has Jesus ever stood between you and your sin? Are there any stumbling stones in your life that need to be unearthed because they threaten to trip up your walk of faith before the Lord?

4. If you were to find yourself in conversation with a Jewish person, how would you convince them that Jesus is their long-awaited Messiah? How can God's promises to Israel be an encouragement to both them and you today?

5. When you hear a teaching that sounds different from what you have learned, what should be your reaction? How can you verify truth? Where do people typically run for answers? To Whom should we go instead?

6. The world builds fortresses to buttress various ideologies and beliefs. How might you recognize these strongholds of deception, and how can you lead someone out of error and to the truth?

7. What building materials are you using to build your spiritual house? Is your house a bastion of truth, or is it housing deception?

8. Who will you impact today with clear truth so they can come to Jesus for salvation rather than stumble over Him on their way toward judgment?

9. If someone were to examine your life, upon what would they say it is built? What place would they say the Cornerstone occupies in your life?

10. What steps are you taking to remove the rocks of offense buried in your life that threaten your fellowship with the Lord and your usefulness to Him?

Matthew 9:1-8

And he entered into a ship, and passed over,
and came into his own city.

And, behold, they brought to him a man sick of the
palsy, lying on a bed: and Jesus seeing their faith said
unto the sick of the palsy; Son, be of good cheer;
thy sins be forgiven thee.

And, behold, certain of the scribes said within
themselves, This *man* blasphemeth.

And Jesus knowing their thoughts said,
Wherefore think ye evil in your hearts?

For whether is easier, to say, *Thy* sins be forgiven
thee; or to say, Arise, and walk?

But that ye may know that the Son of man
hath power on earth to forgive sins, (then saith he to
the sick of the palsy,) Arise, take up thy bed,
and go unto thine house.

And he arose, and departed to his house.

But when the multitudes saw *it,* they marvelled,
and glorified God, which had given such
power unto men.

CHAPTER 3

Are You Bringing People to Jesus?

LOOKING FOR FAITH

Think about sitting in a crowded house listening to Jesus teach when suddenly there is a loud noise on the roof. And that ruckus turns into a gaping hole where an invalid is lowered into the middle of the house. What would you be thinking as this interruption occurred? Would you be annoyed at the disruption, or would your first thought be about what you could do for this infirmed man?

What Jesus noticed was the faith of the one with palsy and the faith of those who brought him. Isn't it nice to know that God notices our faith? The invalid could not walk by himself and needed help. Matter of fact, we all need help at one time or another.

Jesus greets him with one of my favorite statements in the Bible, "Be of good cheer." What a welcome! Jesus wants Christians to be cheerful people because it shows that we trust Him. But cheer seems to be the last thing on the minds of these people. Folks are sick and in need. Jesus immediately

sees the problem and knows the solution. Too often, we forget the God we serve.

I once heard a speaker liken life to a parade. We sit along the street and watch the floats and bands go by. God is up in the Goodyear Blimp and sees the beginning and end of the parade. He sees when the parade turns down the streets. He knows what is coming up. So we should trust Him because He has a much better view from a much better vantage point than we do!

One question that comes up with this passage in Matthew is whether Jesus implies that sin has caused this man's paralysis. Some may be born with such problems, but never, ever forget

Never, ever forget that indulging in sin can wreak havoc on the human body.

that indulging in sin can wreak havoc on the human body. Ever hear someone complain about their ailments, yet both you and they know the tremendous damage they did to their body because they ate, drank, smoked, and drugged their way through the years? Sometimes, people blame God for their condition rather than blame the one staring back at them in the mirror.

But sickness and disease drive us to find answers. They remind us that we will not be on planet Earth much longer. We are just passing through to the other side, so we need to earnestly consider what awaits us there.

Jesus is much more concerned about this man's spiritual condition than about his physical condition. Notice how He addresses him: "Son, be of good cheer; thy sins be forgiven thee." Jesus wants him to know that someone cares for him unconditionally and that there is no reason to lose hope. Jesus knows that even if his palsy lasts his entire lifetime, it is still temporary. It will end the moment he takes his last breath. But Jesus wants to address a deeper and much, much more important issue. By the way, which is worse: being paralyzed or having sin slowly strangle your desire to live?

It probably wasn't even in the universe of anyone's thinking that someone's sins were going to be forgiven that day, but Jesus was willing to forgive this man's sins because He saw their faith. However, this begs the question: Why, when the invalid man was forgiven of his sins, didn't each of the other men jump up and say, *Sir, I want my sins forgiven as well!* Everyone else in the house should have wanted the same.

So how do you look at people? Do you just see their outside appearance, or do you look inside to see if they are lost in sin or born again? How you view people will probably affect how you treat them as well.

THE SKEPTICS

> And the scribes and the Pharisees began to reason, saying, Who is this which speaketh blasphemies? Who can forgive sins, but God alone?
> **Luke 5:21**

Now, we know that only God can forgive sins, so don't miss an important point here. When Jesus forgives this man's sin, He is making Himself equal with God. All sins are an affront to God. We have sinned against Him and Him alone, which is why humans cannot forgive your sins. You can't walk into a confessional and be forgiven. You must go to the one you have offended, and that person is God.

You can't walk into a confessional and be forgiven. You must go to the one you have offended, and that person is God.

> Therefore the Jews sought the more to kill him, because he not only had broken the sabbath, but said also that God was his Father, making himself equal with God.
> **John 5:18**

Yet, many times, people don't go to God for forgiveness. Deep down, they think they have done something unforgivable. I have heard people say, "God can't forgive me for all that I have done wrong." So I ask them, "What is the worst thing you have ever done?" Their answers are amazing. Met a murderer here and there, but most of what they say doesn't seem all that big. Could it be more of a pride issue than anything else? Yes, God can forgive all of those sins, regardless of whether we think they are big or small. Some people think they aren't all that bad, and

since God is good, He will ignore their sin and let them into Heaven anyway. Of course, they forget that a holy God sees all sin as wicked, nasty, and repulsive, and He won't overlook any of it on Judgment Day.

Our thought life matters to God because thoughts lead to actions.

The Scribes didn't miss the implications of what Jesus was saying because "within themselves," they accused Him of blasphemy. Were they so set in their ways that they did not consider the possibility that the Man in front of them might be their Messiah? Were they the know-it-alls of the day who thought they already had the answers to everything?

When Jesus exposed their thoughts, He was letting them in on a little secret: God is standing in front of you! This should have proven His deity to them—and it should totally challenge the worldview of anyone—but the stubbornness and pride of men that wrestles with God rather than obey Him are amazing characteristics.

Our thought life matters to God because thoughts lead to actions. These leaders assumed that Jesus' words were evil, yet Jesus calls out their thoughts as being evil. Forgiving sins would be blasphemous if He wasn't God manifest in the flesh, but if He was, then this was a game changer for the Pharisees and all those within listening distance.

Search me, O God, and know my heart: try me, and know my thoughts: And see if *there be any* wicked way in me, and lead me in the way everlasting. **Psalm 139:23,24**

For the word of God *is* quick, and powerful, and sharper than any twoedged sword, piercing even to the dividing asunder of soul and spirit, and of the joints and marrow, and *is* a discerner of the thoughts and intents of the heart. Neither is there any creature that is not manifest in his sight: but all things *are* naked and opened unto the eyes of him with whom we have to do.

Hebrews 4:12,13

Thou knowest my downsitting and mine uprising, thou understandest my thought afar off. **Psalm 139:2**

The good news is that Jesus does know our thoughts! Yes, I just wrote that. He cares about every little detail of our lives. How much more loving can He be than to care about the minutest thought that someone might have?

Some Jews believed that anyone healed of an illness had to first be forgiven of sins. So Jesus was removing all possible objections and doubt about His identity by healing souls and healing sickness and disease as well.

The pardon comes first, and the healing of the body comes second. And by the way, one of those is needed for eternity and the other is not.

Who forgiveth all thine iniquities; who healeth all thy diseases; **Psalm 103:3**

I said, LORD, be merciful unto me: heal my soul; for I have sinned against thee.

Psalm 41:4

The pardon comes first, and the healing of the body comes second. And by the way, one of those is needed for eternity and the other is not. Yet, so many people would prefer to have the physical healing of their bodies rather than the spiritual cleansing of all of their sins.

THE PROOF

When Jesus asks in verse 5 of our chapter's passage, "which is easier, to say," what is the right answer to that question? *Your*

sins are forgiven is much easier to say. Why? Forgiveness of sins cannot be tested to see if it has actually taken place. But *arise, take up your mat, and walk* can be tested by whether or not the man gets up and walks. If the man does not walk, then Jesus' claims would be false. He would be a laughingstock and a fool in the eyes of the people. But Jesus has all authority, and He executed judgment by executing forgiveness—goodness, graciousness, and mercy all wrapped up in one Man!

And hath given him authority to execute judgment also, because he is the Son of man.
John 5:27

Glorify God! Openly praise Him when wonderful things happen to you. People notice and are intrigued.

When the paralytic was told to take up his bed and walk, it was proof that the physical miracle was happening. He could do neither beforehand. Someone else had to carry his bed. Jesus was showing Himself to be omnipotent. He was showing Himself to be all powerful.

And his fame went throughout all Syria: and they brought unto him all sick people that were taken with divers diseases and torments, and those which were possessed with devils, and those which were lunatick, and those that had the palsy; and he healed them. **Matthew 4:24**

Glorify God! Openly praise Him when wonderful things happen to you. People notice and are intrigued. They have wonderment about this God that you so wholeheartedly trust when you brag about what He has done!

THE MIRACLE

Jesus actually performed three miracles: He forgave the man's sins, He knew the thoughts of the Scribes, and He instantly cured the man of palsy and made him whole again. The external miracle proved that the internal miracle had taken place. All the miracles of Jesus testified that He was sent from God.

Did Jesus perform the miracle before the Scribes and Pharisees had a chance to answer? Sometimes an answer isn't necessary with a good question. Just getting a person to think can be the purpose of asking a question. Make sure to use questions in this way when talking with others. Get them thinking! I always say they have to first think about eternal matters before they can ever become saved.

Notice that the miracle was immediate. The sick man got up and walked. The healing of your sins is immediate, too. Sins are completely washed clean and gone the moment you become born again!

But think about this for a second: When this man picked up his bed, it was proof that the physical miracle had taken place. So when the internal miracle of salvation takes place in someone's life, what is the proof that it has actually occurred? That is right; it is a changed life. It is a life that is lived for the Lord. It

Just getting a person to think can be the purpose of asking a question.

is the life that repents of sin. God is the Potter, and we are the clay. He is shaping and molding us into the men and women He wants us to be, and we want to be pliable in His hands. When people look at you, do they see a life that is being lived for the Lord? Do they see an abundance of God-fruit all over your "tree" of faith? The miracle of a life lived for the Lord is a great thing for the world to behold!

Once when I was speaking in Los Angeles, I got sick. God was gracious to me and let me get through my speaking schedule. By the time I arrived at LAX to return home, I was dreading the four-and-a-half-hour plane flight. I didn't want to talk with anyone; I just wanted to sit down and relax. When I sat down, I looked at the man seated next to me and basically said, *Hi, my name is Mark Cahill. I believe in Jesus, and here is one of the books I wrote. Have a nice flight!* Okay, that wasn't exactly what I said, but that is what I meant by whatever I did say! He replied, "That is interesting." *Oh, no! I didn't want that to be interesting; I wanted to be left alone!* I said, "Why is that interesting?" Well, as you have probably guessed, I didn't get much rest on that flight! He happened to be the director of a TV series called *The Vampire Diaries*. He was flying to Atlanta to film one of the episodes. As we talked, he said he started out as a cameraman and worked his way up to becoming a director. He was a very interesting man. But then he told me that one of the other cameramen he worked with became a Christian and began witnessing to him. He had

listened intently to that cameraman, but he had not made a commitment to Jesus. Then he said that the cameraman could not film certain things anymore because they went against his beliefs.

Don't forget, he was a missionary in Hollywood before ever becoming a missionary in Kenya!

I will set no wicked thing before mine eyes: I hate the work of them that turn aside; *it* shall not cleave to me. **Psalm 101:3**

That cameraman was a man of conviction. He didn't want to set any worthless thing in front of his eyes. That really spoke volumes to this director. That cameraman eventually left the film industry and is now a missionary in Kenya. But don't forget, he was a missionary in Hollywood before ever becoming a missionary in Kenya!

I have planted, Apollos watered; but God gave the increase.
1 Corinthians 3:6

It was nice to come along and water the seed that the cameraman had planted in that director's life. It made it so

much easier to talk with him because he had already met a watchman with conviction.

> Whether therefore ye eat, or drink, or whatsoever ye do, do all to the glory of God.
> **1 Corinthians 10:31**

THE GREATEST DISEASE OF ALL

Jesus is the Master over disease, death, and the power of the unseen. He can do things we can't even imagine. We must trust and have faith in Him at all times.

Speaking of disease, what is the darkest disease of all? That is right: sin. It is the one disease we need to have cured. Now, it will never totally be gone until the other side, but it is the one sickness we must have healed. I would rather have a rickety, old body that doesn't work properly and be forgiven of my sins, than to be an Arnold Schwarzenegger or a Brad Pitt look-alike drowning in the corruption of the world and on the bridge that crosses into an eternal lake of fire.

The Great Internal Physician was standing before the leaders of Israel, but they did not want Him or the cure He offered.

> For the wages of sin *is* death; but the gift of God *is* eternal life through Jesus Christ our Lord.
> **Romans 6:23**

> The next day John seeth Jesus coming unto him, and saith, Behold the Lamb of God, which taketh away the sin of the world.
> **John 1:29**

The wages of sin is death. The consequence of this disease is death. There is nothing more important than finding its cure. The Great Internal Physician was standing before the leaders of Israel, but they did not want Him or the cure He offered. Sadly, the world does not want the cure for sin that God has provided either.

THE SON OF MAN

Interestingly, in verse 6 of our chapter's passage, Jesus makes a direct reference to the book of Daniel by using the phrase *Son of man*. This reference should have gripped the attention of everyone there.

> I saw in the night visions, and, behold, *one* like the Son of man came with the clouds of heaven, and came to the Ancient of days, and they brought him near before him. And there was given him dominion, and glory, and a kingdom, that all people, nations, and languages, should serve him: his dominion *is* an everlasting dominion, which shall not pass away, and his kingdom *that* which shall not be destroyed. **Daniel 7:13,14**

Anyone who does not know the Scriptures can easily get into trouble.

Anyone who does not know the Scriptures can easily get into trouble. Jesus is letting these teachers and leaders know that He is the Messiah—the Son of God—and they are missing it. When He refers to Himself as the Son of man, He is tying Himself to the Scriptures in Daniel that they should have known by heart. By referring to this vision in Daniel, Jesus is also revealing Himself as the Judge!

A NEW LIFE

After the miracle of healing the man's palsy had taken place, Jesus sent him back to his house and back to his family. You wonder if this man's condition had made him a burden to his family, but now, he was coming back as a blessing in many, many ways. You also wonder how many people were saved after he returned home!

Now, never forget how the enemy lies. Society says that special needs or Down syndrome children are not a blessing but a burden, and therefore, it is okay to kill these kids in the womb. No big deal, you can snuff them out and just move on with your life. I have had more than one mom tell me that their special needs child was the biggest blessing to their family. One mom told me that their Down syndrome child has not been easy to raise—there were some tough days— but what a blessing that child has been to everyone in the household. She said she couldn't believe how many moms and dads would abort a blessing that God was trying to give them! Wow, what a statement from a mom.

I've also wondered why some of these supposed healing evangelists don't go to hospitals and ply their trade. Why doesn't Benny Hinn, Todd Bentley, or Reinhard Bonnke walk through the front door of a hospital, go room to room, lay hands on people, and watch them get up and walk out of that same front door? There is a very big reason why they don't do that. Do you know what that reason is?

Always give God the glory, and always be careful of supposed healers who take the glory for themselves.

Why didn't Jesus have the man He healed of palsy go with Him on tour? They could have hit all of the big cities in Israel, attracted some big crowds, and made a fortune. No need. Jesus didn't need the publicity because His fame was already spreading far and wide. Instead, this man needed to go back to his family and tell them about all the things the Lord had done for him.

Always give God the glory, and always be careful of supposed healers who take the glory for themselves. Be watchful of that in any ministry. The praise belongs to God and God alone.

By the way, do you think the man was dancing as he went home? How excited was he? Oh, wait a minute. Was he more excited about having his sins forgiven or about being cured of palsy? That's an interesting thought to consider.

AMAZEMENT

When the multitudes saw the miracle, they marveled. The passage implies they were also afraid. They were caught off guard. Their world was turning upside down. They really didn't expect Jesus to pull off this miracle. *Who was this Man? Where did He come from? Was He really from the Most High God?* Everyone, including the Pharisees and doctors of the law, were amazed, "…We have seen strange things to day" (Luke 5:26).

The miracles were challenging everyone's thinking. They were blowing some brain circuits. Jesus just placed Himself in an entirely different category than anyone they had ever run  across before. The Old Testament makes clear that the Messiah would be a healer. Now that He had fulfilled that prophecy, they had a decision to make about the Man who was standing in front of them.

The miracles were challenging everyone's thinking. They were blowing some brain circuits.

Then the eyes of the blind shall be opened, and the ears of the deaf shall be unstopped. Then shall the lame *man* leap as an hart, and the tongue of the dumb sing: for in the wilderness shall waters break out, and streams in the desert. **Isaiah 35:5,6**

FAITH OR SICKNESS

And said, If thou wilt diligently hearken to the voice of the LORD thy God, and wilt do that which is right in his sight, and wilt give ear to his commandments, and keep all his statutes, I will put none of these diseases upon thee, which I have brought upon the Egyptians: for I *am* the LORD that healeth thee. **Exodus 15:26**

So was all of the sickness within Israel a sign of the spiritual condition of the Jews? By the way, would that apply in the country of America today?

Remember that Jesus is always looking at people's faith. We walk by faith and not by sight. If you want to hear, *Well done, my good and faithful servant* one day from the King, then live your life that way. Strong faith doesn't worry about obstacles or roadblocks but keeps the goal in mind.

A friend of the ministry, who works in the oil fields of Alaska, said that one of his coworkers came into his office just struggling one day. As they talked, my friend let him know, one more time, that without Jesus Christ in his life, he would not be able to handle his circumstances. One problem, his coworker was an atheist! So my friend looked at him, handed him my book *One Heartbeat Away,* and said, "Go to your desk, and just give it thirty minutes."

If you want to hear well done my good and faithful servant one day from the King, then live your life that way.

So the employee went to his desk, read that book for thirty minutes, then walked back into his boss' office and said, "I have never been more wrong about something in my entire life!" When he came in the next day, he told his boss that he got only 45 minutes of sleep the night before because he was reading the book and studying the proofs for God's existence on the Internet.

I ran into that boss man at a church in Texas. He told me that this atheist bought four copies of the book and had already given them to his atheist friends! That is my kind of boss! But better than that, he lives his life by faith. He is a faithful servant of the King, and God uses him in mighty ways.

One last thing to ponder: how did the man who was sick with palsy leave the house? Back through the roof? Nope. It was front-door time for him! Can you imagine the looks on the people's faces as they saw him walk out? *Wasn't he the guy we just saw lowered down through the roof? My, my, what just happened in there?*

Chapter 3
Group Discussion

1. Have you or someone you've known been given a serious wake-up call about the consequences of sin in the light of mortality? How have you met this call by giving out the life-giving hope of the gospel? What was the outcome for having done so?

2. List some of the ways people typically form their views of others. How does looking at external appearances compare with looking at their internal condition? What should be our biggest concern when looking at anyone, and what can we do to address their greatest need?

3. If someone asked you to prove that Jesus is God, how can you use various accounts from the Bible, the words of Jesus, or verses to drive this point home?

4. When the world "reads" your life, what evidences of salvation can they see? Is there enough evidence of salvation in your life to convict you of being a Christian?

5. Has there been a time when either you or someone you know refused the way of escape from sin provided by the Lord? What were or are the consequences for them having done so?

6. Explain how ignoring truth has caused trouble either for you or someone else in the past. How can a thorough knowledge of God's Word protect you or others from difficulties in this life and bring blessings for eternity?

7. Have you encountered someone who either claims to heal or claims to have been healed, only to see them relapse into worldliness or illness? Compare that with someone who has been truly healed by the Lord.

8. Whose life have you been turning upside down, not only with the truth about Jesus, but also with His love and mercy?

9. Describe how truth has been an unstoppable force in your life to push through the lies of the world and to give the lifesaving gospel to the lost. How can this begin to change a nation?

10. How does expressing thankfulness for your salvation impact the lives of both the lost and saved around you?

Matthew 12:33-37

Either make the tree good, and his fruit good;
or else make the tree corrupt,
and his fruit corrupt:
for the tree is known by *his* fruit.

O generation of vipers, how can ye, being evil,
speak good things? for out of the abundance
of the heart the mouth speaketh.

A good man out of the good treasure of the heart
bringeth forth good things:
and an evil man out of the evil treasure
bringeth forth evil things.

But I say unto you,
That every idle word that men shall speak,
they shall give account thereof
in the day of judgment.

For by thy words thou shalt be justified,
and by thy words thou shalt
be condemned.

CHAPTER 4

What is Stored Up in Your Heart?

TREES BEAR FRUIT

One thing we're all familiar with is the law of cause and effect. Actions cause reactions. Things are related and linked to one another. Jesus is making the same point here. A bad tree produces bad fruit; a good tree produces good fruit. An evil heart produces evil things; a good heart produces good things.

The Scribes and Pharisees are accusing Jesus of evil, so He challenges them to make a decision. Either His works show that He truly is the Son of God, or His works and miracles are from the devil. One or the other. Stand up for what you believe. No middle ground. Decide who Jesus is and tell others about Him.

While doing prison ministry work one time, I started a conversation with an inmate. He had worked for the Mafia back in New York but was incarcerated in a Florida prison. He told me that he was serving a thirteen-year sentence for smuggling marijuana by boat. I said, "That must have been a big boat!" He said, "It was two boats!" If you lie, cheat, and steal, don't be surprised if you end up running drugs one day. Evil produces evil, and good produces good.

> As saith the proverb of the ancients, Wickedness proceedeth from the wicked: but mine hand shall not be upon thee.
>
> **1 Samuel 24:13**

> Enter not into the path of the wicked, and go not in the way of evil men.
>
> **Proverbs 4:14**

Generation of Vipers

To call these leaders a generation of vipers is to call them out in very strong terms. Jesus is definitely not giving them a compliment. He is saying their evil goes back a long time. The

term *viper*, or *serpent*, takes us back to the Garden of Eden. This wickedness has gone on for many, many generations. Are these leaders doing what their fathers and grandfathers did? Have their long-standing religious traditions given them permission to act like serpents? If so, then who in this lineage will break the cycle of evil? Who will come to Jesus for a new heart so that generations afterward will have a chance to be different?

Have their long-standing religious traditions given them permission to act like serpents?

> Therefore the Lord shall have no joy in their young men, neither shall have mercy on their fatherless and widows: for every one *is* an hypocrite and an evildoer, and every mouth speaketh folly. For all this his anger is not turned away, but his hand *is* stretched out still.
>
> **Isaiah 9:17**

The leaders challenging Jesus are not neutral by any stretch of the imagination. He is hitting them hard by calling them a generation of vipers. He isn't playing games. He is inferring they are corrupt. He is inferring they have bad character. He is inferring they are wrong and have been wrong for a long time. He is warning them that they need to repent and move away from evil immediately.

But many people don't want to move away from the traditions of their fathers. Instead, they would rather make themselves comfortable in the religious traditions they are familiar with, even when those practices are false. Many traditions gloss over sin and promise salvation to all—that is, to all who don't challenge the authority or false beliefs within that system. Jesus was definitely challenging both the authority of the Jews and the status quo.

Speaking of false beliefs, Henri Nouwen, the Roman Catholic mystic, once said, "Today I personally believe that while Jesus came to open the door to God's house, all human beings can walk through that door, whether they know about Jesus or not. Today I see it as my call to help every person claim his or her own way to God."[26] Mr. Nouwen is apparently very indecisive about Jesus being the only way to Heaven. He seems to think that people can believe whatever they want to believe, and they will be okay when they die. And, of course, Jesus gives a strong, resounding *no* to that foolishness.

Jesus saith unto him, I am the way, the truth, and the life: no man cometh unto the Father, but by me. **John 14:6**

Everyone needs to investigate Scripture to see if what Jesus says is correct, because if His words are true, then we can only come through Him to be right with the Father.

You see, the words of Jesus make you thirsty. His words should have had that effect on the Pharisees, and they should have that effect on us today. Everyone needs to investigate Scripture to see if what Jesus says is correct, because if His words are true, then we can only come through Him to be right with the Father. Strong statements like these cause people to search out whether Jesus is speaking truth or not.

HISSING SOUNDS

Watch a YouTube video about serpents and notice what you hear—a hiss. That hiss means the snake will keep its distance from you, and you should keep your distance from it. Snakes are typically more afraid of us than we are of them, but, of course,

Listen to those around you. People are laying their real cards on the table.

we don't know that! Therefore, we should never drop our guard. What do you hear from someone with a wicked heart? Bitterness. Anger. Yelling. Screaming. Hatefulness. Cursing. Just listen to those around you. People are laying their real cards on the table. They are letting you know who they have been serving with their lives. And don't forget, their words are a window to their true heart. Sometimes their anger—the hiss—makes

us want to keep our distance from them. Other times, we may want to know what is causing their pain so we can give them the truth they need to have a new heart through Jesus Christ.

> Ye are of *your* father the devil, and the lusts of your father ye will do. He was a murderer from the beginning, and abode not in the truth, because there is no truth in him. When he speaketh a lie, he speaketh of his own: for he is a liar, and the father of it.
>
> **John 8:44**

These Jewish leaders knew the book of Genesis, and they knew what happened in the Garden. Taking these generations all the way back, it seems that Jesus is comparing them to Satan. Again, these are strong words. The Jews are not missing what He is saying, and He doesn't want them to miss the point either. So, He goes for the heart. He hits them hard because He wants them to think. He wants a response. What response does He want from all people? Repentance and belief!

Israel was well acquainted with the hiss of these vipers. These religious leaders laid heavy burdens on the people without lifting a finger to ease their load. They loved to be revered, yet they shut men out of the kingdom of Heaven. They ignored the weightier matters of the law, devoured widows' homes, and took for themselves the gifts that should have been dedicated to God. They prayed for show and decorated the tombs of the "religious fathers" who murdered the children of God. They even traveled land and sea to convert others to their hypocritical practices. They were corrupt and blind guides who ignored the law, justice, mercy, and faith. Indeed, they were vicious snakes who slithered among the children of God, biting, infecting, and poisoning them with their traditions of evil.

Israel was well acquainted with the hiss of these vipers. These religious leaders laid heavy burdens on the people without lifting a finger to ease their load.

For the vile person will speak villany, and his heart will work iniquity, to practise hypocrisy, and to utter error against the LORD, to make empty the soul of the hungry, and he will cause the drink of the thirsty to fail.

Isaiah 32:6

Out of the same mouth proceedeth blessing and cursing. My brethren, these things ought not so to be. Doth a fountain send forth at the same place sweet *water* and bitter? Can the fig tree, my brethren, bear olive berries? either a vine, figs? so can no fountain both yield salt water and fresh.

James 3:10-12

Regarding generations, when I was a school teacher back in the day, we had parent-teacher night. It was always a long but interesting evening! During one conference, I recall meeting the parents of an 8th grade student of mine named Jeff. When I met his dad, something clicked. Jeff was the spitting image of his father. He looked like him, had similar mannerisms, and even used some of the same words. It hit me hard that the apple doesn't fall far from the tree. Kids, in many respects, turn into their parents, whether that is good or bad.

Overflowing Heart

Whatever abundance is stored up in our hearts will spill out of our lives sooner or later. If you have wickedness and evil locked up in your heart, these will eventually overflow at some point.

Whatever abundance is stored up in our hearts will spill out of our lives sooner or later.

But those things which proceed out of the mouth come forth from the heart; and they defile the man.   **Matthew 15:18**

One day, I decided to wash my clothes. Mom taught me to do that years ago, and periodically, I follow her advice! So I turned on the washer and went downstairs. A little while later, as the washing machine was pushing water out of the drum, the toilet downstairs started overflowing like Niagara Falls! I went running upstairs, hit the OFF button on the washer, and a few seconds later, everything calmed down. They do the same with Niagara Falls, believe it or not. They can shut off the Falls, and everything stops.

So what do you do when you are clueless about these things? Call your dad, of course! Well, Pops told me I needed a plumber in a hurry. I called a friend who is a plumber, and he came over, sized up the situation, and said, "You need to call the county." So, I did. A few hours later, some trucks and six guys arrived. They checked the pipes, and in five minutes

they assessed the problem and said, "You've got roots." I said, "What are you talking about? This is a semi-new place. That little small tree in the front yard hasn't been there that long." He looked at me and said again, "Roots!" He let me know that roots will grow toward the nearest water source. Well, the nearest water source was the pipe in front of my house!

Roots had caused a blockage in the pipes, so when the washing machine dispensed all of that water into the pipe, there was nowhere for it to go. It took all of the gunk, junk, and funk that had backed up in there and overflowed it into my bathroom and onto the carpet! It was lovely. I mean really, really lovely! It wouldn't have been a big deal if it was just clean water, but it wasn't—it was dirty and nasty. The cleanup was not fun at all.

By the way, if you had an overflow of your heart today, what would come flying out of it? Anger, bitterness, hatred, or lust? Or would it be forgiveness, love, peace, and joy?

By the way, if you had an overflow of your heart today, what would come flying out of it? Anger, bitterness, hatred, or lust? Or would it be forgiveness, love, peace, and joy?

It really depends, doesn't it? If you have connected to the evil side, we know what would be gushing out. But if you have a new heart and the Holy Spirit is in control, we know what would be flowing out of there as well.

STOREHOUSE

Words are always from the overflow of the heart. Whatever has been stored inside a person's heart is rising up to the top and coming out.

Keep thy heart with all diligence; for out of it *are* the issues of life.

Proverbs 4:23

"Men's language discovers what country they are of, likewise what manner of spirit they are of. The heart is the fountain, words are the streams. A troubled fountain, and a corrupt spring, must send forth muddy and unpleasant streams. Nothing but the salt of grace, cast into the spring, will heal the waters, season the speech, and purify the corrupt communication. An evil man has an evil treasure in his heart, and out of it brings forth evil things. Lusts and corruptions, dwelling and reigning in the heart, are an evil treasure, out of which the sinner brings forth bad words and actions, to dishonour God, and hurt others. Let us keep constant watch over ourselves, that we may speak words agreeable to the Christian character."[27]

Treasure up eternal things in this life and not the temporary things of the world.

So the good treasure of the heart is love toward God and man, and the bad treasure is the carnal mind, hatred, and ill will toward God and man. So make sure you have treasured up some great, godly things in your heart. Don't strive after the treasures of man. None of those treasures will ever make it with you when you move on over to the other side. Treasure up eternal things in this life and not the temporary things of the world.

The Scribes and Pharisees had just accused Jesus of blasphemy, which God takes very seriously. They tried to condemn Jesus with their words, but those words condemned them by exposing the true condition of their hearts. It seems their infidelity had carried them so far away from God that they didn't realize they needed to repent of those words.

Thou shalt not take the name of the LORD thy God in vain: for the LORD will not hold *him* guiltless that taketh his name in vain.

Deuteronomy 5:11

We really do live in interesting days. Kobe Bryant was once fined $100,000 for calling a referee a faggot. One hundred grand! That is a lot of money. But we live in a day and an age where you dare not utter a gay slur, or you will be in trouble with the word police. What is very intriguing to me is reading the lips of coaches and players during games. They say "Jesus Christ" and "God d*****" as curse words all the time. It is a daily occurrence in the NBA and other pro sports organizations. Did you think it was appropriate when the NBA fined that coach $200,000 for using a Christian slur? Well, of course you didn't because it never happened! You can curse the God who created you every day of the week

The God who wrote Deuteronomy 5 will ask many, many people why they took His gorgeous, beautiful, glorious, and forgiving name in vain, as if it had no value.

in the NBA, and no one cares. Not even a blip on the screen. But remember, all idle words will be brought to account with God. The God who wrote Deuteronomy 5 will ask many, many people why they took His gorgeous, beautiful, glorious, and forgiving name in vain, as if it had no value.

WORDS MATTER

Jesus says that "by thy words thou shalt be justified, and by thy words thou shalt be condemned." *Justified* is the opposite of *condemned*. Remember, all words matter to God. Don't ever, ever forget that.

> That if thou shalt confess with thy mouth the Lord Jesus, and shalt believe in thine heart that God hath raised him from the dead, thou shalt be saved. **Romans 10:9**

Your words will either acquit you or convict you. So when you're in a court of law, do you want to be found guilty or

innocent of all charges? That is why the police, at times, will tap someone's phone or have someone wear a wire to a meeting. They are trying to get suspects to incriminate themselves and admit to their wrongdoing. But if the person never admits to the act, then it is possible they never committed the crime. Words are powerful.

> Death and life *are* in the power of the tongue: and they that love it shall eat the fruit thereof. **Proverbs 18:21**

Whenever someone sits on a witness stand, you listen intently. You pay close attention to what they are saying. You try to find out if they are being truthful. *Can I trust what they are saying?* You are looking for their intentions as well. *Does this person have a score to settle? Does this person have a relationship of some sort with the defendant and want to see them go free?* All of that comes into play when you are trying to decipher what they are really saying.

Police, at times, will tap someone's phone or have someone wear a wire to a meeting. They are trying to get suspects to incriminate themselves and admit to their wrongdoing.

When sitting on a jury, you always want to hear from the defendant. You want to hear their words. The one time I was actually on a jury, I really, really wanted to hear from the defendant. I wanted to watch his face. I wanted to hear the inflection in his voice and pay attention to his exact words. I had my pad of paper and pen ready to go in case he took the stand. Now in this trial, he didn't take the stand. As a juror, you do not in any way hold that against him. The prosecutor has to prove his case—that is their job. But when it was time for us to find the defendant guilty or not guilty, I really wish we could have heard from him. That is the power of words.

Even media headlines try to sway our thinking by the words they use or don't use, like pro-life or anti-abortion. Those terms have very different connotations and embed very different messages because words are powerful.

So, can you pick out those smooth talkers who are just trying to get a dollar out of your pocket? Can you tell when someone you are chatting with has an agenda? Can you tell by someone's words if they do or do not really care about you?

Never look at words as a trivial matter. The words in this book took a lot of work—and I do mean a lot—before going to print to make sure it glorifies the Lord. God used words to speak creation into existence, and He used words to write out His intentions in the

If God is going to judge my idle words, what is He going to do with the evil and wicked things I have said? Thank goodness for the cleansing blood of Jesus Christ!

Bible. And remember, Jesus is the Word become flesh! All words matter to God!

INVESTING WITH WORDS

The Lord is letting us know in our chapter's passage that we will be accountable for all of our idle words. Words that just sit there with not much meaning to them. Words that do not build up in truth or destroy untruths. Now think about that for a second. If God is going to judge my idle words, what is He going to do with the evil and wicked things I have said? Thank goodness for the cleansing blood of Jesus Christ!

> Set a watch, O LORD, before my mouth; keep the door of my lips.
> **Psalm 141:3**

We need to pray for the Lord to stand guard at the door of our mouths. We should also be ready to heed His warnings not to let certain things pass across our lips. We should be watchmen who guard the truth and guard the souls of men, but how can that be if I am talking about sports, the opposite sex, money, academics, politics, gossip, and/or cursing with the breath He has given me?

> Neither filthiness, nor foolish talking, nor jesting, which are not convenient: but rather giving of thanks. **Ephesians 5:4**

For in many things we offend all. If any man offend not in word, the same *is* a perfect man, *and* able also to bridle the whole body.

We do not want to speak useless or idle words because our words count. They should build others up and not tear them down.

Behold, we put bits in the horses' mouths, that they may obey us; and we turn about their whole body. Behold also the ships, which though *they be* so great, and *are* driven of fierce winds, yet are they turned about with a very small helm, whithersoever the governor listeth. Even so the tongue is a little member, and boasteth great things. Behold, how great a matter a little fire kindleth! And the tongue *is* a fire, a world of iniquity: so is the tongue among our members, that it defileth the whole body, and setteth on fire the course of nature; and it is set on fire of hell. For every kind of beasts, and of birds, and of serpents, and of things in the sea, is tamed, and hath been tamed of mankind: But the tongue can no man tame; *it is* an unruly evil, full of deadly poison. **James 3:2-8**

We do not want to speak useless or idle words because our words count. They should build others up and not tear them down. They should lift others up and not destroy them.

> The heart of the wise teacheth his mouth, and addeth learning to his lips. **Proverbs 16:23**

Chapter 4

> Let no corrupt communication proceed out of your mouth, but that which is good to the use of edifying, that it may minister grace unto the hearers.
> **Ephesians 4:29**

Remember, your heart is a storehouse, and whatever things you are investing in yourself will one day come flowing out of you. And those overflowing words will impact those around you.

At a friend's house one day, his four-year-old daughter had a curse word come flying out of her mouth. My friend just laughed and laughed and laughed. I guess he thought it was pretty funny. I was not as impressed. So I asked, "Who did she learn that word from?" No response. "Where did she first hear that word?" Well, she first heard that word from her dad! I let him know so. He knew I was right. He had invested that curse word in her storehouse, and there it came tumbling across her lips one day in front of other people.

Remember, your heart is a storehouse, and whatever things you are investing in yourself will one day come flowing out of you.

We need to always keep in mind that we answer to the Lord. He is the One to whom we will give an account on Judgment Day for how we lived this life. Are you living with this perspective in mind? Only the Lord can give you a "thumbs up" for a life well lived for Him. Keep pleasing Him with all that you do and say as you get ready for that day, which will be coming in the very near future.

> So then every one of us shall give account of himself to God.
> **Romans 14:12**

Words are a big, big deal to God. They show the true condition of the heart: Good versus evil. Selfless versus selfish. God versus Satan. Who is winning the war for your heart?

Chapter 4
Group Discussion

1. Biblically speaking, what are the characteristics of good and bad trees? How can they appear to be similar, and how can they be distinguished from one another?

2. If you have come out of a false belief system, name some of the bad fruit which accompanied that tradition. What broke that cycle from repeating itself in your family or circles of influence? How are you warning others to avoid the same deception?

3. What role do words play in hooking the heart to sin and evil? Whose words should we trust and why? What standard do we use to distinguish truth and goodness from error and evil?

4. When people claim there is more than one way to get to Heaven, what do their words reveal about their faith? How can you spice up a conversation so they might rethink their ideas and start searching for truth?

5. Who is the father of sin, lies, and murder? How do you defend God's character against accusations of causing evil and sin?

6. What are some examples of idle words and speech? What kinds of words should we speak with the breath we've been given? What kinds of words honor the Lord?

7. Give examples of how people take the name of God in vain. What accountability will they bear on Judgment Day? What warnings do those who love Jesus Christ want to give them?

8. How does corrupt speech expose the heart? How does it defile a person? What steps should you take to correct this in yourself or in others when it surfaces?

9. Are there any weeds in your heart that shouldn't be allowed to grow? What steps can you take to pull out those weeds by the roots to make your heart a fountain of life and truth?

10. Is your heart moved with compassion for the lost, those in prison, and the downtrodden? How can you let the heart of Jesus Christ flow through you today to bless them with truth and encouragement?

Matthew 23:29-39

Woe unto you, scribes and Pharisees,
hypocrites! because ye build the tombs of the prophets,
and garnish the sepulchres of the righteous,

And say, If we had been in the days of our fathers, we would not
have been partakers with them in the blood of the prophets.

Wherefore ye be witnesses unto yourselves,
that ye are the children of them which killed the prophets.

Fill ye up then the measure of your fathers.

Ye serpents, *ye* generation of vipers,
how can ye escape the damnation of hell?

Wherefore, behold, I send unto you prophets, and wise
men, and scribes: and *some* of them ye shall kill and crucify;
and *some* of them shall ye scourge in your synagogues, and
persecute *them* from city to city:

That upon you may come all the righteous blood shed
upon the earth, from the blood of righteous Abel
unto the blood of Zacharias son of Barachias,
whom ye slew between the temple and the altar.

Verily I say unto you, All these things
shall come upon this generation.

O Jerusalem, Jerusalem, *thou* that killest the prophets,
and stonest them which are sent unto thee, how often
would I have gathered thy children together, even as a hen
gathereth her chickens under *her* wings, and ye would not!

Behold, your house is left unto you desolate.

For I say unto you, Ye shall not see me henceforth, till ye
shall say, Blessed *is* he that cometh in the name of the Lord.

CHAPTER 5

Who Holds the Keys to Your House?

NAME-DROPPING

The righteous men of the past had a rock-solid faith. They stood for truth and didn't back down, even in the face of persecution. In fact, they were willing to die for their faith rather than turn away from the truth or pervert it. Their deeds showed they loved God more than their own lives. These are the righteous saints of God we want to identify with and honor.

Apparently, the Pharisees wanted to identify with them, too, since they honored their memory and decorated their tombs. By laying claim to the righteous martyrs of the past, they gave the impression that they were of the same faith as them, but was that really true?

The Pharisees seemed to pay more attention to these tombs and sepulchers than to the teachings and lives of the prophets inside. But don't you find the same to be true today? People seem much more concerned about the outward adornment of others than with their inner faith and depth of character.

In ancient Israel, part of the Temple offerings given by the Jews went toward maintaining the tombs of the prophets. One good thing to know is where your money goes after you give it away. Prior to speaking at an Episcopal Church conference in Cincinnati one time, I found out that some of their tithes were being given to Planned Parenthood, an organization that murders babies. When I mentioned this to a few of the people there, they had no clue this was happening. After some quick research, they discovered for themselves that it was true. Make sure you know what your money will be supporting before you give it away.

What is it that truly lasts? Your character will last. Investing in other people's lives will last. Your words will last.

Yet, all of the artwork on the tombs of the prophets would eventually fade away. Go to a cemetery sometime and notice the older tombstones. Look at the inscriptions of names and dates that are weathered and fading away. What is it that truly lasts? Your character will last. Investing in other people's lives will last. Your words will last. All of these have a ripple effect that will continue into eternity, whether good or bad.

The deceased prophets of the past left behind a legacy of faith that lasted, but the Pharisees were leaving a different history behind. They may have adorned the tombs of the dead prophets, but they did not honor or heed the living prophets of their own day! The irony is fascinating to think about.

John the Baptist was the prophet who prepared the way for the Messiah, but the Pharisees disregarded his message. Jesus Christ was the Prophet whom Moses foretold would come, but the Pharisees didn't listen to Him either. By rejecting Jesus, they were basically saying they were self-sufficient and did not need the Messiah. They thought they could be right with God without Him.

CHAPTER 5

These hard hitting words of Jesus in our chapter's passage are the last of eight woes that He pronounced on Israel's leaders. Such strong warnings should have gripped their attention, but they were deluded. Their pride had risen so high. Rather than rebuke the murderers who killed the prophets, the Pharisees called them their fathers! And like them, they could kill the prophets; and if need be, they could kill Jesus, too.

HYPOCRITES

In the Bible, the word *hypocrite* shows up 33 times. Interestingly, *hypocrite* was a common Greek term for an actor who worked behind a mask. Stage players in antiquity wore masks to hide their true identity as they played the part of their characters.

We live in a society today where people are paid millions of dollars to be hypocrites. A friend of mine, before he passed away, built movie sets for a living. Many movies are filmed on studio lots, but these designed sets are not the reality you might think they are when watching a movie. Actors and actresses play the part of someone they really are not. The better they are at pretending or lying, the more convincing they will be as an actor, and typically, the more money they make. I rarely darken the door of a movie theatre because I don't want to give those liars my money, and I don't want to support the totally ungodly world of Hollywood. This is also why I don't own a television. I don't want my cable or satellite fees funding that wicked industry.

In the time of the Greeks, it was easy to figure out the real identity of the actors. You could walk up to them, take off their masks, and see their faces. Jesus is doing the same here. He is unmasking the Pharisees. He is showing us their real character. He is revealing their true colors. Don't live a lie. Don't be a hypocrite. It is not a healthy way to go through life, and you will have regrets when the time of unmasking comes.

The Pharisees gave the impression they would have not have been partakers with the fathers in killing the prophets and would have been innocent of bloodshed, but since they are about to turn Jesus over to be crucified, I am not so sure I trust their words. They are about to do something much worse than killing the prophets; they are about to reject and murder the Son of God.

If you deny Jesus in your actions now, what makes you think you would not have denied Him then?

Sometimes, we think we know what we would do in a situation, but really, we cannot be sure until we cross that bridge. If someone came into your church with a gun right as your Sunday school class was studying this book, are you 100 percent sure what you would do? When adrenalin starts flowing, we may not always act in the way we think we would in a given situation.

Some of us think we would never have denied Jesus like the people did back then. Are you sure about that? If you deny Him in your actions now, what makes you think you would not have denied Him then?

Think about yourself for a moment. If you had been living back then, would you have been yelling *crucify Him*, or would you have been fighting for Him? Or would you have very cowardly slithered away and blended in with the crowd without making your stand known for the King? Be careful. If you will not stand up for Jesus Christ in your workplace, witness to lost people while you are out and about, or hand out tracts on the streets, then don't be so sure of your answer.

Also consider the very sobering statement of Jesus in our chapter's passage, "the measure of your fathers." Total and complete judgment is coming. The Pharisees are so sure they would never have killed the prophets of the past, but so many of them were acting just like their long lost relatives. By doing so, they were fitting themselves for the coming Judgment.

Jesus sure seemed to have a good set of enemies, and some of them even wanted to kill Him. Why? He was nowhere near being a hypocrite. He stood solidly for His Father and spoke the truth plainly. Jesus had a big list of enemies, yet His life was well lived for His Father.

It is okay to have enemies. Matter of fact, you should have some enemies in your lifetime. Sometimes people say you can judge others by their enemies. If you are living a true and holy Christian life, not everyone is going to like you. That is normal. They treated your Savior the same way.

> Woe unto you, when all men shall speak well of you! for so did their fathers to the false prophets. **Luke 6:26**

Churchill's dictum shows the truth of Jesus' teaching:

> "You have enemies? Good. That means you've stood
> up for something, sometime in your life."
> **—Winston Churchill**[28]

> Blessed are ye, when *men* shall revile you, and persecute *you*, and shall say all manner of evil against you falsely, for my sake. **Matthew 5:11**

If we're standing strong for the Lord Jesus Christ and the truths of God's words, we will have enemies. That is okay. Now, if people don't like you because you are a jerk or unloving, that is another story. I always tell people to speak the truth in love, and let the chips fall where they may. Make sure you spend more time worrying about being a friend of Jesus than worrying about whether friends and strangers like you down here.

FATHERS

Have you heard the saying, *like father like son?* It's more true than people might realize. How many times have you met an alcoholic whose father was an alcoholic as well? You see, fathers set the tone for the entire family. They set the course that many of their children will follow, which means the influence of a biblical father can never be underestimated. So

if you have a bad pathway behind you, make the choice to get off of that dead-end track, change directions, and get on the right path before it is too late.

So if you have a bad pathway behind you, make the choice to get off of that dead-end track, change directions, and get on the right path before it is too late.

Thou shalt not make unto thee any graven image, or any likeness of *any thing* that *is* in heaven above, or that *is* in the earth beneath, or that *is* in the water under the earth. Thou shalt not bow down thyself to them, nor serve them: for I the LORD thy God *am* a jealous God, visiting the iniquity of the fathers upon the children unto the third and fourth *generation* of them that hate me; And shewing mercy unto thousands of them that love me, and keep my commandments. **Exodus 20:4-6**

A gentleman who had read *One Heartbeat Away* emailed me one day. He said he was a WWII veteran. He made the fatal error of putting his phone number in his email, so I called him! We had the neatest chat. He was a machine gunner at the Battle of the Bulge! I told my mom that I had history on the telephone. So I picked his brain for a while.

He said he had seen a copy of *One Heartbeat Away* lying on a table at a VA hospital and perused it a bit. He also told me he loves to read, so he figured that if it was left on the table, then he could take it! When he emailed me, he had already read the book once and was half way through it for the second time. He said, "I have three hundred years of Catholicism in my family. After reading this book, I am now trusting Jesus Christ, and Jesus Christ alone, for my salvation." All I could say was, "Wow!" Then he said, "My mind is sharp as a tack. I love to read. You got any more books?" Well, we sent him everything I had at that time. In his next email, he let me know that he

had read *One Heartbeat Away* three times through, front to back, and he was telling everyone he could about Jesus! If you live in Ohio, there is an 89-year-old evangelist roaming around, so you better watch out!

This veteran made the decision to break the cycle of Catholicism in his family. No more rituals. No more good works to get to Heaven. No more, *I hope I get there.* No more infallibility. He is trusting in the blood of Christ, and nothing else, for the washing away of his sins. He now wants everyone else to have that same blessing as well!

SENDING

As a good Father, God, in His grace, wants everyone to have the truth. He wants them to have the right information so they will commit their lives to Him. He sent the Jewish people prophets of truth, but what did their fathers do? Rather than listen to them, they killed them! Think about that for a second. What would you do if your friends kept killing your emissaries? Would you send them your only child to finally get their attention? I doubt many of us would, but our all-loving, merciful, and gracious God thinks differently than

As a good Father, God, in His grace, wants everyone to have truth.

we do. He sent His Son to the Jews, and they put Him to death, but that death became the sacrifice for the sins of the world.

Very interestingly, in verse 34 of our chapter's passage, where Jesus talks about the righteous men they will kill, He says, "I send." One more time, He is making the claim that He is God. Don't miss it. Only God can send out prophets. This means God is in their presence, and the Pharisees don't even realize it.

> In the year that king Uzziah died I saw also the LORD sitting upon a throne, high and lifted up, and his train filled the temple. Above it stood the seraphims: each one had six wings; with twain he covered

his face, and with twain he covered his feet, and with twain he did fly. And one cried unto another, and said, Holy, holy, holy, *is* the Lord of hosts: the whole earth *is* full of his glory. And the posts of the door moved at the voice of him that cried, and the house was filled with smoke. Then said I, Woe *is* me! for I am undone; because I *am* a man of unclean lips, and I dwell in the midst of a people of unclean lips: for mine eyes have seen the King, the Lord of hosts. Then flew one of the seraphims unto me, having a live coal in his hand, *which* he had taken with the tongs from off the altar: And he laid *it* upon my mouth, and said, Lo, this hath touched thy lips; and thine iniquity is taken away, and thy sin purged. Also I heard the voice of the Lord, saying, Whom shall I send, and who will go for us? Then said I, Here *am* I; send me.   **Isaiah 6:1-8**

By the way, do you have that same attitude? *God, please send me anywhere and everywhere to do your bidding. Put the right people in front of me so I can explain eternal truth to them. God, please make sure that I explain the cross and salvation accurately to those I meet.* God is in the sending business. He wants to send you and me to do His bidding. Are you available to the King to be sent and used by Him today?

By the way, do you have that same attitude? God, please send me anywhere and everywhere to do your bidding.

Jesus knows they are going to kill some of His prophets, but He sends them anyway. He cares for the Jewish people and wants to give them every opportunity to repent.

Therefore also said the wisdom of God, I will send them prophets and apostles, and *some* of them they shall slay and persecute: **Luke 11:49**

Then said Jesus to them again, Peace *be* unto you: as *my* Father hath sent me, even so send I you.   **John 20:21**

Sadly, this would be a precursor for the ages to come. The prophets of God were killed before the cross, and many soldiers of Christ would die after the cross as well. Only at the Second Coming of the King will evil be stopped and the world be set right.

KILLING AND CRUCIFYING

To kill and crucify is a wicked thing to do. It is cruel. It is vicious. It is a terrible way to live one's life. Visit a prison sometime, and you'll see man after man and woman after woman who have thrown away their lives by the evil deeds they have committed. Who would want to kill anyone, let alone a prophet of God? Think about the heart of these people.

As I am writing this book, police officers are being assassinated in different parts of America. Just go and talk with some officers today. Ask them if they have ever fired their gun in the line of duty. Not only have most of them never done that, they never want to do that either! I have met very, very few officers who have

Only at the Second Coming of the King will evil be stopped and the world be set right.

answered yes to that question. They want a nice, simple day on the streets and then to go home to their families. They do not wake up in the morning looking for someone to shoot and kill.

There are so many false teachers out there today. So many of them mock the name of God. Many false religions destroy the name of Jesus, but do I want to hunt any of them down and kill them? Of course not! I pray for them. I pray for someone to witness to them with eternal truth. I take the opportunity to talk with them whenever we cross paths. That is what we as Christians do.

Yet, these Pharisees are hell-bent on destruction. It seems to be their calling card. God is trying to keep people in line with love, but they are trying to keep people in line with fear and control. What a contrast.

This pattern of murdering the prophets has been going on throughout the ages. Those who do so are part of the generation of vipers. They are the offspring of serpents. They slither and hiss and nip at the heels of the believers. Do you hear them? Do you see them? They are looking for a good bite. Do you obey them, or do you wear some good steel-toe boots covered in the blood of Christ so those serpents don't stand a chance against you?

OVERFLOWING EVIL

It seems that each generation can add to the evil of the generation before it. Very few seem to break the cycle to side with truth. They keep pouring a little bit more into the cup of evil until, finally, the cup is full and literally overflowing everywhere. Look at our world today. Look at the obvious decadence of our culture. Go talk to someone with some white hair on their head, and ask them what it was like to be alive fifty, sixty, or seventy years ago. Have them compare life back then to life today. It is shocking to realize how the cup of evil is overflowing all across our world at this time in history.

> But in the fourth generation they shall come hither again: for the iniquity of the Amorites *is* not yet full. **Genesis 15:16**

The cup of the fathers' evil was filling to the brim. One more drop, one more evil act of killing *the* Prophet—their Messiah—and the cup would overflow. That critical drop would hit the cup very shortly, as they turned Jesus over to be crucified. That tipping point was literally so momentous that it was like tossing in a bag of ice cubes, which caused spillage to overflow everywhere for the Jews. It released a tsunami of trouble for putting their Messiah to death. Betraying Jesus would prove to be very costly for the Jewish people.

> And God said, Let us make man in our image, after our likeness: and let them have dominion over the fish of the sea, and over the

fowl of the air, and over the cattle, and over all the earth, and over every creeping thing that creepeth upon the earth. **Genesis 1:26**

Those who killed the prophets would now be the ones who would kill the Christ. Those who were created in His image and to be the apple of His eye would now be the ones who would put Him to death! This is utterly fascinating to think about.

PERSECUTING THE INNOCENT

Thinking you are innocent of murder when you didn't actually commit the crime doesn't exonerate you. When the Jews handed Jesus over to the Romans to be killed, they were just as guilty as the executioners. Even if you don't have the abortion but pay for it, you are just as guilty.

> And Cain talked with Abel his brother: and it came to pass, when they were in the field, that Cain rose up against Abel his brother, and slew him. And the LORD said unto Cain, Where *is* Abel thy brother? And he said, I know not: *Am* I my brother's keeper? And he said, What hast thou done? the voice of thy brother's blood crieth unto me from the ground. **Genesis 4:8-10**

Don't think you can shed innocent blood, and it will escape the notice of the Lord.

Don't think you can shed innocent blood, and it will escape the notice of the Lord. Don't think you can take the life of a baby, in or out of the womb, and the King doesn't care. Don't think a nation can murder over 50 million babies, and God will just sit on the sidelines. He has patience for those who repent and mercy for those who do right, but severe judgment awaits those who keep poking their fingers in His eye.

A nation will pay for the blood it has spilled. How about a nation that loves war too much? I met an older guy on a plane flight to Fort Myers, FL, one time. He was from Germany. He said to me, "You Americans love war too much." He recalled that as a kid, he used to play in bombed-out buildings during and after WWII. I used to play on jungle gyms in school-yards! The spilling of blood leaves a treacherous impression on those who have suffered because of it.

People forget that holiness has to judge. It has to separate the holy from the unholy. It creates a line of demarcation between the children of God and those in rebellion against Him. Which side of the line are you on?

Violent reactions can erupt from those who reject the conviction of sin.

And the Spirit of God came upon Zechariah the son of Jehoiada the priest, which stood above the people, and said unto them, Thus saith God, Why transgress ye the commandments of the LORD, that ye cannot prosper? because ye have forsaken the LORD, he hath also forsaken you. And they conspired against him, and stoned him with stones at the commandment of the king in the court of the house of the LORD. Thus Joash the king remembered not the kindness which Jehoiada his father had done to him, but slew his son. And when he died, he said, The LORD look upon *it,* and require *it.* **2 Chronicles 24:20-22**

Violent reactions can erupt from those who reject the conviction of sin. Zechariah spoke truth on behalf of the Lord and was murdered, on the spot, to silence that conviction. As a priest, Zechariah was permitted to enter the Temple to offer sacrifices for sin, yet Joash the king sacrificed him in the Temple as a display of his rebellion.

And in her was found the blood of prophets, and of saints, and of all that were slain upon the earth. **Revelation 18:24**

Jesus sees all the bloodshed committed against the righteous as coming from one source. Those who murder God's prophets are aligning themselves with the lineage of serpents. They are part of the generation of vipers who are guilty of all the blood spilled on the earth in the long war against God. Jesus points to the beginning of martyrdom that began with Abel and the last prophet martyred in the Old Testament, Zacharias, son of Barachias, to make the point that murdering one is the same as murdering them all. Anyone who murders one of God's children becomes guilty of the entirety of bloodshed committed against the servants of God.

Jesus further explains to the Pharisees that their ilk will scourge God's children—who speak truth—in their synagogues and persecute them from town to town. Can you imagine meting out punishment within the walls of your church? What about killing someone inside of your church? This is how far people can go when they are not saturated with the love

*Anything is possible
when you are
not walking very
tightly, hand in hand,
with the Lord.*

of God through the Word of God. Anything is possible when you are not walking very tightly, hand in hand, with the Lord. Satan just needs some breathing room between you and the King so he can slip through and create a chasm of separation.

> But when he saw many of the Pharisees and Sadducees come to his baptism, he said unto them, O generation of vipers, who hath warned you to flee from the wrath to come?   **Matthew 3:7**

Individual Scribes, Pharisees, and Sadducees could have repented and walked away from the killing of Jesus. They could have walked away from the example set by their fathers. They could have walked away from persecuting the children of God. They each had an individual choice to make, just as all men have that same choice to make today. The generation of vipers, who persecute the children of truth, has continued from the first century even up until now. When will it finally end?

> Take, my brethren, the prophets, who have spoken in the name of the Lord, for an example of suffering affliction, and of patience.
> **James 5:10**

By the way, where are the powerful voices of God's people today who are calling out the evils of the church and the world? Where are the people who are trying to shut you down because you speak so strongly for the Lord? Make sure you are telling the world enough truth that it either hates you or heeds your message to believe.

Ye adulterers and adulteresses, know ye not that the friendship of the world is enmity with God? whosoever therefore will be a friend of the world is the enemy of God.   **James 4:4**

Make sure you are telling the world enough truth that it either hates you or heeds your message to believe.

But how can we warn the world if we are just like them? No need to be a friend of the world. You won't be here for very long, and everything it offers is perishing. You are just here for a moment of time before passing through to the other side.

And said to the mountains and rocks, Fall on us, and hide us from the face of him that sitteth on the throne, and from the wrath of the Lamb: **Revelation 6:16**

The punishment for the evil of persecuting the innocent and putting to death the children of God has been simmering and bubbling up like lava in a volcano. All that people have needed to do through the years is repent and return to the Lord. God has given us a simple plan, and many have rejected it. The magma is rising. A blast of epic proportions is coming. The wrath of the Lamb is drawing near, and the world is not ready for that day. What are you doing to prepare folks for the Judgment to come?

DESTRUCTION IS COMING

The cross was rapidly approaching. Jesus knew the crucifixion was at hand. He had proven that He was the Messiah by raising the dead, restoring sight to the blind, curing leprosy, and much more. His wisdom was profound and unparalleled. He spoke truth and pointed the way to His Father. But for all of His teachings, miracles, and warnings, Israel refused to be gathered to her Savior.

Decision time had arrived, and it would soon pass by. Either come to Messiah for salvation or reap ruin and desolation. With their final moment to repent slipping away, He pronounces the consequences of their unbelief.

> And when he was come near, he beheld the city, and wept over it,
> **Luke 19:41**

Jesus loved the Jews and Jerusalem then, and He loves the Jews now. He knew trouble was on the horizon. He warned them again and again. Sadly, they had brought it upon themselves, and it brought Him to tears. He wept over the city of Jerusalem because He knew what was coming for those who would reject Him.

Do you also love the Jews? When you have the opportunity, do you tell them about their Savior and how to be saved? Do you tell them how to escape the condemnation of Hell? I have a friend who goes to Israel every year just to witness to the Jews. She loves the Jews! She wants all of them to know *Yeshua haMashiach*: Jesus the Messiah!

"During the three years of our Lord's public ministry, his preaching and miracles had but one object and aim, the instruction and salvation of this…disobedient people. For their sakes, he who was rich became poor, that they through his poverty might be rich: for their sakes, he made himself of no reputation, and took upon him the form of a servant, and became obedient unto death, even the death of the cross! He died, that they might not perish, but have everlasting life. Thus, to save their life, he freely abandoned his own."[29]

The Jews' unbelief had separated them from Jesus. He would always be with them, but His relationship with them

would be very different. They had no idea about the trouble that awaited them. In a short forty years, the destruction of Jerusalem would come at the hands of the Roman general Titus. Trouble was coming, and it would be strong. When God says He will do something, He will do it. But He was so

gracious to give the Jews time to be born again by the blood of Jesus Christ before that destruction arrived.

When God says He will do something, He will do it.

Looking back over the last 2,000 years, Israel's rejection of their Messiah has brought them untold heartache. All they had to do was repent and believe in their King! But one day, the nation of Israel will repent, and what a joy it will be to behold!

He shall cover thee with his feathers, and under his wings shalt thou trust: his truth *shall be thy* shield and buckler. **Psalm 91:4**

But unto you that fear my name shall the Sun of righteousness arise with healing in his wings; and ye shall go forth, and grow up as calves of the stall. **Malachi 4:2**

Jesus shows His heart as He laments, "O Jerusalem, Jerusalem." He held out His arms to His people time and time again, longing to gather and protect them, but in their rebellion, they would not come to Him. They ignored the eternal consequences for turning away from Him.

"The metaphor which our Lord uses here is a very beautiful one. When the hen sees a beast of prey coming, she makes a noise to assemble her chickens, that she may cover them with her wings from the danger. The Roman eagle is about to fall upon the Jewish state—nothing can prevent this but their conversion to God through Christ—Jesus cries throughout the land, publishing the Gospel of reconciliation—they would not assemble, and the Roman eagle came and destroyed them. The hen's affection to her brood is so very strong as to become proverbial."[30]

Jesus was about to enter Jerusalem, the city where prophets went to die. The Sanhedrin, the great council, could condemn someone to death and hand them over to the Romans to carry out the execution. This is literally Jesus' final farewell to the city. The curtain is coming to a close.

THE DESOLATED HOUSE

The generation of vipers has taken over God's house. Jesus is the rightful owner, yet He is leaving the House of Israel and the Temple and will not return until the end of days. The Jews didn't recognize Him when He was standing before them, and they wouldn't realize when He was absent from them. Their house was being left desolate because Jesus would no longer be in it.

Anywhere that Christ is not present turns into a wilderness. Weeds grow. Sin abounds. The enemy breaks in, steals, kills, and destroys. Look around and see how the devil is ravishing the world. Make sure that does not happen in your life or to those around you.

Think about whether Jesus has left your home or church. Is He knocking on the door, but you cannot hear Him? Pride is an amazing thing. It can convince you that God is not in front of you when He is actually right before your eyes. It can convince you that you are in right standing with Him when you are actually still in sin.

Anywhere that Christ is not present turns into a wilderness.

I will go *and* return to my place, till they acknowledge their offence, and seek my face: in their affliction they will seek me early.

Hosea 5:15

Blessed *be* he that cometh in the name of the LORD: we have blessed you out of the house of the LORD. **Psalm 118:26**

And so all Israel shall be saved: as it is written, There shall come out of Sion the Deliverer, and shall turn away ungodliness from

Jacob: For this *is* my covenant unto them, when I shall take away their sins.   **Romans 11:26**

The Jews should have believed their Scriptures. They should have recognized their King. Jesus says He will not return to them until they seek His face. They need to acknowledge their sin, and say, "Blessed is he that cometh in the name of the Lord."

Jesus has always been the Watchman to the Jews. His loving, gracious, and caring heart longed for their souls to be right with Him. But free will has one major downside: it gives you the freedom to reject the One who gave you the free will to love and adore Him. By the way, are you being a watchman to the Jews? If not, why not?

But free will has one major downside: it gives you the freedom to reject the One who gave you the free will to love and adore Him.

I was in the Newark Airport recently and struck up a conversation with a Jewish man named Meir. He was heading to a Jewish wedding in Israel. As we were talking, he told me he believed that many gods became one God, Yahweh. Yahweh then became the God-man, Jesus. And ultimately, all of us will end up being gods! Okay, do you see anything wrong with his theology? Yikes! What an interesting talk we had. Do you care enough about the Jews to strike up a conversation with them and tell them the truth?

> Jerusalem hath grievously sinned; therefore she is removed: all that honoured her despise her, because they have seen her nakedness: yea, she sigheth, and turneth backward.   **Lamentations 1:8**

> For the children of Israel shall abide many days without a king, and without a prince, and without a sacrifice, and without an image, and without an ephod, and *without* teraphim: Afterward shall the children of Israel return, and seek the LORD their God, and David their king; and shall fear the LORD and his goodness in the latter days.   **Hosea 3:4,5**

> But my people would not hearken to my voice; and Israel would none of me. So I gave them up unto their own hearts' lust: *and* they walked in their own counsels. **Psalm 81:11,12**

The national abandonment of the King of Israel was now final. Jerusalem had sinned grievously, and now persecution, affliction, and tribulation awaited them. Individual Jews could repent, but the nation as a whole had turned its back on their Messiah. But always remember that Jesus delights in the repentance of sinners! He loves it!

True repentance brings godly sorrow. It mourns for the sins committed against the Lord.

The time was at hand. The consequences for not coming to the King were inevitable. The nation would see Jesus as a criminal hanging on the cross, but they would not come to Him as their Messiah, the Light of the World. They had chosen to side with darkness, and now it would become very dark for them in the centuries to come.

> And I will pour upon the house of David, and upon the inhabitants of Jerusalem, the spirit of grace and of supplications: and they shall look upon me whom they have pierced, and they shall mourn for him, as one mourneth for *his* only *son,* and shall be in bitterness for him, as one that is in bitterness for *his* firstborn. **Zechariah 12:10**

True repentance brings godly sorrow. It mourns for the sins committed against the Lord. Israel's rejection of Jesus has been costly, but one day, the lost sheep of the house of Israel will come home! The house of David will cry out for their Shepherd, and He will return to them.

What a way to end His public ministry—an open-armed plea to come to Him for protection from judgment. He knew the pain their rejection of Him would bring. He showed them their sin and invited them to be saved! What compassion! What love for those who had offended Him! What a Savior!

Chapter 5
Group Discussion

1. How do people today "decorate" the tombs of religious men from the past? How should we be adorning the empty tomb of Jesus instead?

2. Give examples of how Christians can pay more attention to the outward trappings of Christianity, theologies, and the teachings of men rather than give attention to their inward walk with the Lord and reaching the lost.

3. List some of the traits that true men of God exhibit and compare them to the behaviors displayed by those who reveal themselves to be hypocrites. Who do you think is watching us to see if we are living a true or hypocritical Christian life?

4. What examples have been set for you by your own father concerning the Christian faith? Is it an example worth emulating or an example that needs correcting?

5. Did the "generation of vipers" come to an end in Jesus' day, or has it continued to the present time? Name some of the characteristics that mark those who dwell in the lineage of serpents as compared to those who abide in the line of faith. Explain why bloodshed against the righteous is seen as coming from one source.

6. What does your earnest contending for the faith show those who oppose or persecute you? Is it possible for their opposition or persecution to back you down from declaring the gospel or your faith in Jesus Christ?

7. Give examples of how you have seen the cycle of false religious traditions broken inside of a family. What challenges did that family face, and what was the outcome in the end?

8. How is someone still guilty of transgression by encouraging sin, not speaking against sin, standing on the sidelines, or going along with the crowd while sin is taking place?

9. How have you seen both non-Christians and Christians become angry when convicted of sin? What should be the reaction of Christians when confronted about their sin or when falsely accused of sin? What do these reactions reveal about their faith?

10. What investments are you making with your life that will last into eternity? What return on those investments will the Lord and others reap? How does this focus help us to better invest our time, talents, and resources during our brief time on Earth?

Luke 6:46-49

And why call ye me, Lord, Lord,
and do not the things which I say?

Whosoever cometh to me,
and heareth my sayings, and doeth them,
I will shew you to whom he is like:

He is like a man which built an house,
and digged deep,
and laid the foundation on a rock:
and when the flood arose,
the stream beat vehemently upon that house,
and could not shake it:
for it was founded upon a rock.

But he that heareth, and doeth not,
is like a man that without a foundation
built an house upon the earth;
against which the stream did beat vehemently,
and immediately it fell;
and the ruin of that house was great.

CHAPTER 6
Are You Digging Deep?

MASTER AND LORD

If we are calling Jesus, *Lord, Lord,* then He is our Master. He is the One to whom we answer. He is our Leader. Simple as that. Wait a minute, though. Why do we call Him *Lord, Lord,* yet not do the things He tells us to do? Shouldn't we have a godly fear of the One we call *Lord, Lord?*

> A son honoureth *his* father, and a servant his master: if then I *be* a father, where *is* mine honour? and if I *be* a master, where *is* my fear? saith the LORD of hosts unto you, O priests, that despise my name. And ye say, Wherein have we despised thy name? **Malachi 1:6**

The implication here is that we are literally despising the name of God by not obeying what He tells us to do. Those are strong words. They are meant to be strong words. Reread that verse from Malachi again. Those are very, very strong words.

> When once the master of the house is risen up, and hath shut to the door, and ye begin to stand without, and to knock at the door, saying, Lord, Lord, open unto us; and he shall answer and say unto you, I know you not whence ye are: Then shall ye begin

to say, We have eaten and drunk in thy presence, and thou hast taught in our streets. But he shall say, I tell you, I know you not whence ye are; depart from me, all ye workers of iniquity.

Luke 13:25-27

The tongue tells me what is in your heart, but your deeds tell me what you really believe.

Workers of iniquity do not obey the Lord—it is as clear as a bell. Obedience is very big in the eyes of God. When you read your Bible straight through from Genesis to Revelation, you will notice that obeying God jumps off the pages all over the place.

Be careful of just paying lip service to Jesus. He can see right through it. You might have others fooled, but you don't have Him fooled. The tongue tells me what is in your heart, but your deeds tell me what you really believe. You don't want to be someone who says one thing but does another.

If you walk it but don't talk it, you are just a good person. Folks like that are everywhere. They are a dime a dozen. If you talk it but don't walk it, you are a hypocrite. Those folks aren't too difficult to find either. But if you walk it and talk it, you are the most dangerous person on planet Earth! Satan couldn't move you with a bulldozer if he tried!

When people claim Christianity but don't take their faith seriously, they're playing what I like to call a *Get Out of Hell Free* game—just repeat some words to God that you think will guarantee biblical salvation, hope those words will stop you from going to Hell, and then just go and live any way you want. If all of your intentions were insincere and you are just going through the motions, you know it and God knows it. This is not a game. This is serious business. It is serious anytime you are dealing with the King.

Ask yourself, why would you live this way? Why would you do it? Cut out the charades. Either drop all the pretenses and

live for Christ, or give up Jesus and go live in the world. Make your decision. Quit straddling the fence. As one of my friends once said, "Satan owns the fence." Either live for Jesus or live for the world. Time is up. Make your decision.

Think about the personal affront it would be to tell your parents that you love them, love them, love them, but then refuse to comply with their requests. What if they asked you to take out the trash and clean your room over and over again, but you never did it. I think they would begin to question whether you really love them since you won't obey them. Think about the personal affront it is to Jesus if in our churches or in our prayers we say we love Him, but we show no proof of that love in our lives. What if someone critiqued our lives and found no evidence of a true relationship with Jesus Christ? It begs the question: Do we truly love Him?

People thought they believed in Him, but have they really followed Him in their heart?

The term *Lord, Lord* is used five times in the Bible. It is not an overused term. Look up each of those references, and pay very close attention to how the term is used. People are calling Him *Lord, Lord* because they claim to be believers. Jesus has drawn big crowds. People thought they believed in Him, but have they really followed Him in their heart?

> Not every one that saith unto me, Lord, Lord, shall enter into the kingdom of heaven; but he that doeth the will of my Father which is in heaven. Many will say to me in that day, Lord, Lord, have we not prophesied in thy name? and in thy name have cast out devils? and in thy name done many wonderful works? And then will I profess unto them, I never knew you: depart from me, ye that work iniquity. **Matthew 7:21-23**

> This people draweth nigh unto me with their mouth, and honoureth me with *their* lips; but their heart is far from me. **Matthew 15:8**

The Scribes and Pharisees said they loved God with their lips, but their actions showed something far different. Jesus is warning people here. He is specifically warning His followers to not—under any circumstances—act like hypocrites. Believers are different. We are bought with a price. Lip service doesn't cut it. Our whole lives are to be given to Jesus. No one will regret it now or when we meet Jesus on the other side!

> "If Jesus Christ be God and died for me, then no sacrifice can be too great for me to make for Him."
> —C. T. Studd[31]

If ye know these things, happy are ye if ye do them. **John 13:17**

But be ye doers of the word, and not hearers only, deceiving your own selves. **James 1:22**

For lack of a better illustration, Christianity isn't a spectator sport; it's a participation sport. You want to get off of the sidelines and get in the game. You are supposed to participate in Christianity. It is not an intellectual exercise. It is time for action. Make sure you have an active faith and not an inactive one.

UNMOVABLE FOUNDATION

Jesus is about to clearly explain to the Jews what He means by hearing and doing His sayings. He is going to make it very simple for them so they don't misunderstand His words. This is the kindness of Jesus coming through. He doesn't want anyone to miss this point.

Jesus is telling this parable in Galilee, and the Galileans would have been very familiar with the winter runoff and spring rains that caused the rivers to rise and overflow their banks. These floodwaters deposited a mixture of sand and rocks on either side of the channel creating a near-level plain of debris. After the heat baked the floodplain into pavement, someone might be fooled into thinking it was an ideal location

for building a house. But when the torrents returned the following spring, the house wouldn't stand a chance against the heavy slurry of water mixed with gravel that would sweep the valley floor again. The house would collapse because it was built on nothing more than loose ground.

To build a good foundation, you have to dig deep. You want to put those pillars deep down in the ground and anchor it to rock. The deeper they are set, the sturdier the building will be. The World Trade Center buildings were built to withstand a hurricane. The buildings could sway in heavy winds, but they would not topple over. Why? They had the proper foundation. Some buildings in earthquake zones are even built on rollers! Yes, you read that correctly. They roll from side to side when the earth shakes, which prevents the building from collapsing.

Keep in mind that as we serve the Lord, we must dig deep. We need to be in the Scriptures. To be a leader, you have to be a reader! We need to turn off our phones and soak up some good teachings. We need to talk about the things of the Lord with believers. Keep digging deep. There are treasures to be found in the truth of God's Word that will build us up and help us to reach the lost.

Trust ye in the LORD for ever: for in the Lord JEHOVAH *is* everlasting strength:
Isaiah 26:4

We need to be in the Scriptures. To be a leader, you have to be a reader.

Rest assured that God is our strength. God is our Rock. God is the only foundation that will keep us standing strong as we live this life.

That they do good, that they be rich in good works, ready to distribute, willing to communicate; Laying up in store for themselves a good foundation against the time to come, that they may lay hold on eternal life. **1 Timothy 6:18,19**

When we come to Jesus in spirit and in truth, we are building on the right foundation. Then we want to stack up good and godly works on the foundation of Christ all the days of our lives.

BOMBPROOF FOUNDATION

Many times when buying a house, you take a careful look at the concrete slab it's sitting on. It can tell you a lot about that home's future. Any good builder will tell you about the importance of laying a proper foundation for any building project they work on.

I live in a place called Stone Mountain, GA. Stone Mountain is the largest piece of exposed granite in the world. It was the setting for my book *Reunion*. When you stand next to that granite mountain, you are in awe of its size. I was out there the other night, and I felt very small! Stone Mountain is immovable. The granite above ground is part of a larger body of rock below the surface which extends for miles and miles. Stone Mountain has a foundation that makes it immovable, at least to men. All God has to say is *move*, tap it with His finger, cause a nice earthquake, and suddenly, Stone Mountain becomes very, very movable!

If you detonate dynamite on it, some of that granite would break off. If you set off a nuclear bomb, it would destroy much of that beautiful mountain. The obstacle that prevents it from being completely destroyed is its foundation. Its foundation is so deep. Its foundation is so strong. They say its foundation reaches seven miles down and all the way into North Carolina! You can mess with the top part of Stone Mountain, but its foundation is not going anywhere unless God says so!

Likewise, if you want to live your life correctly for God, you must—and I do mean must—have an immovable foundation. That foundation must be so completely solid that no matter what circumstance comes into your life, you will not be moved.

CHAPTER 6

Therefore, my beloved brethren, be ye stedfast, unmoveable, always abounding in the work of the Lord, forasmuch as ye know that your labour is not in vain in the Lord.   **1 Corinthians 15:58**

And did all drink the same spiritual drink: for they drank of that spiritual Rock that followed them: and that Rock was Christ.
1 Corinthians 10:4

Since you must have the right foundation, you need to make sure that your foundation is made of rock. Christ is that Rock. A life committed to Him and lived according to His ways is a life that Satan will never be able to destroy.

For other foundation can no man lay than that is laid, which is Jesus Christ. Now if any man build upon this foundation gold, silver, precious stones, wood, hay, stubble; Every man's work shall be made manifest: for the day shall declare it, because it shall be revealed by fire; and the fire shall try every man's work of what sort it is. If any man's work abide which he hath built thereupon, he shall receive a reward. If any man's work shall be burned, he shall suffer loss: but he himself shall be saved; yet so as by fire.   **1 Corinthians 3:11-15**

Your works will be tested and rewarded one day. You don't want to be empty-handed in the place you really retire.

Your works will be tested and rewarded one day. You don't want to be empty-handed in the place you really retire. Test yourself here. Get rid of the junk in your life, and do the things that God has commanded you to do. Then there will be nothing to fear the moment you meet the King.

The wicked are overthrown, and *are* not: but the house of the righteous shall stand.   **Proverbs 12:7**

By the way, who would build a house without a foundation? That would be pretty foolish, wouldn't it? Why even start the project? Why waste the money? Who would draw up architectural plans without including a foundation? So, why live your life without a foundation either? Why watch your kids live that way? I just met a 19 year old the other day who told me he didn't grow up with any religious foundation. His parents were just going to let him search it out and decide for himself. I will be very clear here, that is an unbiblical way to raise children. And why let your coworkers who do not have the foundation of Christ just pass you by, day in and day out, when you can tell them how to have the proper foundation for their life now and for eternity?

STANDING OR FALLING

Think about building your dream home. This is the home you have always wanted. If you believe in retirement, this is the home you will live in until your last breath. Remember, when you turn 65, you don't retire, you refire! You have fewer days to live for the Lord down here. Time to get busy!

Remember, when you turn 65, you don't retire, you refire! You have fewer days to live for the Lord down here.

So if you were building this dream home, would you build it on sand or on rock? Now if it is my dream home, I want sand beyond the front door so that I can witness to people on the beach! But I do not want to lay the foundation of my house on that beach. My goodness, the sand on beaches can't even hold umbrellas in place when a little wind pops up. No way would I build my dream home on shifting sands!

I love walking into the homes of righteous people. You can recognize, very quickly, if that home is built on the Rock of Christ. You will also notice things in the home that let you know it is committed to the Most High God. Make sure your house is righteous in the days to come, and you will be just fine.

I have to be honest: I don't have a TV. I haven't had cable for over 20 years, and it has been a blessing. But I do like to watch videos about weather—one of those idiosyncrasies I have. I can watch tornado and flood videos all day long! There is something about the power of those events that just captivates me. Now don't get me wrong, I never want to reach out with my hand and ever touch a tornado or a flood. No, thank you! But sometimes, I can't take my eyes off of those pictures and videos.

Go look at some video footage of a flood—maybe one of those strong, powerful Mississippi River floods. It is unstoppable. It is headed your way no matter what you do to try and stop it. Truth from your lips and from your church should be the same in your school, workplace, family, and city—literally unstoppable.

Are you flooding your city with truth? Are there so many gospel tracts being handed out that everyone is hearing truth? Has every door been knocked on in your city?

Are you flooding your city with truth? Are there so many gospel tracts being handed out that everyone is hearing truth?

Flooding isn't the only storm event that can knock a house over. Wind and rain, which Jesus mentions in the parallel account in Matthew 7, can do the same. See, forces can work over time to weaken a house and bring it down. Wind and rain can loosen a home from its foundation well before the structure ever falls. I always tell people that you just don't wind up in jail all of a sudden. It was a little lie here and a little theft there. Then it was a bigger lie and a bigger theft until the next thing you know, you are down for twenty years because of armed robbery! I do prison ministry work. I talk to prisoners. That is exactly what happens. Smoke a joint here. Take a drink there. Skip work for the first time next. Hang out with the wrong crowd later. And that path led them to a jail cell. Life isn't that difficult to figure out. By the way, what path are you on?

In the same way, someone doesn't just walk away from their faith all of a sudden either. Satan wants to put them on the slippery slope of immorality, partying, listening to worldly music, or challenging authority. He gives them a little bad doctrine here, an offense there, not reading their Bible next, or leads them to a worldly church later; and pretty soon, the walls of their house can come crashing down. But God wants you to fortify your house with truth so you can stand strong against the tide of sin.

God wants you to fortify your house with truth so you can stand strong against the tide of sin.

Thus saith the LORD, Stand ye in the ways, and see, and ask for the old paths, where *is* the good way, and walk therein, and ye shall find rest for your souls. But they said, We will not walk *therein*.   **Jeremiah 6:16**

As I was writing this book, I saw an article that got my attention. There is a newly built, $350 million high-rise in San Francisco that is beginning to sink and shift. Some high-dollar clients who bought condos in this high-rise are not happy. The architect and builder say the building is fine. But the building has already sunk sixteen inches! Turns out, the city was doing some major underground construction in the area nearby, and now they are being accused of creating conditions that caused the building to shift. This is a good reminder here. Other things can mess up your foundation. Be careful. Satan might be making a move for the foundational elements of your life. If he can get to your foundation, he can literally get your whole life to topple over.

Go into a neighborhood and look at two houses that seem similar. They might even be exact copies of one another, but if they were built on different foundations, you might want to own only one of them. The strength of your foundation matters. Likewise, the composition of your spiritual foundation matters, too.

SIFTING AND SHIFTING

The next time you are sharing your faith at the beach, stoop over and pick up some sand. Watch as it runs through your fingers back down to the other grains of sand. Now pick up a rock. That rock isn't going anywhere until you decide to drop it.

Remember, your foundation needs to be built on the true Rock. Never, ever drop the Rock of Christ. Never, ever walk away from Him. He is your solid foundation for all of eternity. By the way, are there any cracks in your foundation that need repairing? Is there anything you need to repent of to get back in right relationship with the Rock today?

When the storms of life hit, the house that is built on sand will collapse. It might be a dream mansion, but it will not hold up. It doesn't stand a chance against the forces that beat upon it, and it will collapse in devastation and great ruin.

Is there anything you need to repent of to get back in right relationship with the Rock today?

Always keep in mind that you do not want devastation on the day you stand in front of God at the Bema Seat Judgment for believers. You want your life to count. God wants to reward you well for a grand life lived for Him!

PASSING THE TEST

Our real self is who we are on the inside, which people can't see. It will be tested. That test usually comes through the difficulties of life. Those moments build character. The Potter is shaping the clay. We may go through a hard time, but there is a beautiful life that will be coming out on the other side!

That the trial of your faith, being much more precious than of gold that perisheth, though it be tried with fire, might be found unto praise and honour and glory at the appearing of Jesus Christ:

1 Peter 1:7

Trials and testing are okay. They will make you so much more Christ-like in the days to come! You want a faith that has been tested and tried because that is the type of faith that will be rewarded.

Knowing *this,* that the trying of your faith worketh patience. But let patience have *her* perfect work, that ye may be perfect and entire, wanting nothing. **James 1:3,4**

So test yourself. Put yourself through the rigors of comparing your life with the people of faith you find in the Bible. See how you stack up, so to speak. Ask a friend if they see anything in your life that doesn't line up with the Bible.

Do the testing now, and you will be ready when the storm hits.

Study to shew thyself approved unto God, a workman that needeth not to be ashamed, rightly dividing the word of truth.

2 Timothy 2:15

The important thing to remember is you must show yourself approved unto God, not man. That is the key.

For do I now persuade men, or God? or do I seek to please men? for if I yet pleased men, I should not be the servant of Christ.

Galatians 1:10

Nevertheless among the chief rulers also many believed on him; but because of the Pharisees they did not confess *him,* lest they should be put out of the synagogue: For they loved the praise of men more than the praise of God. **John 12:42,43**

The important thing to remember is you must show yourself approved unto God, not man. That is the key. Too many of us are people pleasers instead of God pleasers.

So where have you placed your security? In what are you trusting? Who or what has become the bedrock of your life? A flood of epic proportions is coming, and you must be ready.

FLOODWATERS RISING

If a flood came rushing through your town and you had that nice stone house up on the hill, you would hate to see the devastation of others below, but you and your family would be okay. However, if you had a cabin that sat right by the river's edge, and you didn't know that the recent days of rain were moving a surge of water downstream toward your house, you might feel secure, but you would actually be in danger. Trouble is coming, but you just don't see it yet.

The same is true of the flood that is coming with the reckoning of the Lord. Payment time is coming. Your life is going to be judged, whether good or bad. You still have days left to store up treasures in the heavenlies. Might as well go for it, before it is too late.

Your life is going to be judged, whether good or bad. You still have days left to store up treasures in the heavenlies.

> But if ye will not do so, behold, ye have sinned against the LORD: and be sure your sin will find you out. **Numbers 32:23**

If your life is based on the foundation of sin or if your life is based on the foundation of doing nothing for the Lord, trouble is coming. You will not be able to stand when the winds and rains of righteousness come. First of all, make sure you are born again and saved. Second of all, get rid of the dross in your life. Cast anything that is worthless to the wayside. Live holy and fully for the Lord with your remaining days!

Also, if you know what you should be doing and are not doing it, be careful. You are playing with fire. You are playing with a coming flood of judgment. You can't win at that game.

You do not want great ruin in your life now or in eternity. Heed the call today, before it is too late.

Those who ignore the warnings will suffer. All of their work, all of their long days, and all of their efforts in building their house will come to great ruin. What a waste. Don't waste your life! One more time, *DON'T* waste your life!

What could be more ruinous than one soul—just one—that goes off into the afterlife without hope? When you see pictures or videos of terrorist attacks, is your first thought about where those souls will end up for eternity? Are you concerned about one more soul that is not ready to meet Jesus? Does that bother you? Does it bother you that someone around you does not have truth and is not ready to meet their Maker? Does it bother you enough to do something about it?

What could be more ruinous than one soul—just one—that goes off into the afterlife without hope?

As I mentioned earlier, I like weather videos. Probably the most fascinating ones I've seen have been of the Japanese tsunami. I couldn't believe some of the footage. The power of that water stunned me. The devastation throughout parts of Japan blew me away. Those who went to higher ground were fine. Many had only minutes to get to safety. Some buildings were swept off their moorings, and other structures never even budged. You could hear the creaking and groaning of homes and buildings as they were being crushed. The audio was stunning. Some structures weren't going to make it. The sounds from those buildings indicated that in a very short time, they would be gone. Life is like that, too. Sometimes the bad back, the creaky knees, the bad report from the doctor, gray hair, or no hair reminds us that our days are numbered. But also, do you hear the creaking, the breaking, and the cries of lost souls around you? Some people in the tsunami videos were trying to outrun the waters; some made it, and some did not. Some were helping others, and some were not. In one video, I saw some people reaching out to help an older lady before the oncoming waters took her away. Some people went up on the mountainside and watched it all play out. The water wouldn't rise that high or move that mountain. Some were more concerned for their own safety, and some were more concerned about the safety of others. In which category would you have been?

Your spiritual house will be tested by trials, persecutions, and judgment. The superficial building will fall, but the legitimate structure will stand.

> Be not deceived; God is not mocked: for whatsoever a man soweth, that shall he also reap. **Galatians 6:7**

> And he stretched forth his hand toward his disciples, and said, Behold my mother and my brethren! For whosoever shall do the will of my Father which is in heaven, the same is my brother, and sister, and mother. **Matthew 12:49,50**

> The fruit of the righteous *is* a tree of life; and he that winneth souls *is* wise. **Proverbs 11:30**

Very simply, are you building your life on the true and rock-solid foundation of Christ? Are you building on that foundation with the precious truths of God? Is your house of faith strong enough to withstand the brute force of floodwaters pushing felled trees and debris against your house? Is your foundation so firmly anchored to Christ that no catastrophe could move you, no matter what the circumstances? And are you doing the will of the Father in Heaven by winning souls for the Lord Jesus Christ so that others can stand, not only against the trials in life, but also in the Judgment to come? Will you do that for Him and for the lost, before it's too late? Judgment Day is coming, and everyone must be ready to face that day and to stand before the Son of Man.

Chapter 6
Group Discussion

1. Who is being deceived when we do not live out our faith by obeying the Lord? Who suffers as a result? How does this affect you, other Christians, the lost, and the Lord, both now and in eternity?

2. What kind of faith is Jesus commending and warning against in our chapter's passage (Luke 6:46-49)? To what does Jesus equate hearing but not doing? What is the end result of someone who hears the Word but does not do the things He asks them to do?

3. What kinds of "lip service" do people pay to Jesus? When they don't mean what they say, who is really being deceived? Who is not fooled by their empty words?

4. What destiny will someone reap who accumulates knowledge and good works, yet builds on a false foundation?

5. If we examined the bedrock of your life, what would we find as the driving force behind all you think, do, and say? What foundation is your life really built upon?

6. What basic practices of the Christian faith can we use to build and maintain a strong foundation in Christ?

7. Have you inspected your spiritual foundation recently for cracks or wear? Are there any changes in your life that need to be made to shore up those weaknesses? How will these changes become a normal part of your life?

8. How important is evangelism to the Lord? What provisions for saving the lost has He made? Who is the Lord asking and sending to tell the world about the gospel of salvation? Are you complying with His command to preach the gospel to all creatures?

9. When serious trials have hit in your life, who were you able to reach for Christ because of that trial? Did your rock-solid faith make a difference in how they listened to the truth and the gospel you shared with them?

10. Knowing that your life is going to be tested by fire, what focus should you have as you go through your days? Is it possible for Christians to be ashamed and suffer loss when their life is judged? What deeds should you engage in so that the review of your life by the Lord will be smooth and rewarding?

Luke 15:1-7

Then drew near unto him all the publicans
and sinners for to hear him.

And the Pharisees and scribes murmured,
saying, This man receiveth sinners,
and eateth with them.

And he spake this parable unto them, saying,

What man of you, having an hundred sheep,
if he lose one of them, doth not leave
the ninety and nine in the wilderness,
and go after that which is lost, until he find it?

And when he hath found *it,*
he layeth *it* on his shoulders, rejoicing.

And when he cometh home,
he calleth together *his* friends and neighbours,
saying unto them, Rejoice with me;
for I have found my sheep which was lost.

I say unto you, that likewise joy shall be
in heaven over one sinner that repenteth,
more than over ninety and nine just persons,
which need no repentance.

CHAPTER 7
Are You on a Search and Rescue Mission for Christ?

GLIMMER OF HOPE

This passage tells us the tax collectors and heathens drew near to Jesus. These sinners probably felt far away from God, like they had ruined their lives and were beyond hope, yet they flocked to Jesus. Why did they do that? They knew He had something they needed, and He received them affectionately. He cared about them. He showed them, and all people, the same kind of love that He expressed when John laid his head on His bosom. Don't miss the absolute love that Jesus has for everyone.

So we see the Creator of the universe reaching out with truth and love to the people who, in the depravity of their sins, are farthest away from Him. By the way, the word *universe* can be broken down into *uni* and *verse*. *Uni* means "single," and *verse* means "sentence." So *universe* means "single sentence." What is the first verse in the Bible? Genesis 1:1: "In the beginning God created the heaven and the earth." So when anyone mentions the word *universe*, they are actually talking about the very first verse in the Bible! Most of the time, they don't even realize it.

Study the actual words of Jesus. He was a strong, strong speaker. He shot straight, and He shot hard, yet people drew near to Him. They weren't afraid of Him. They were intrigued by Him. Some drew near because they wanted to hear more of His teachings. Others drew near to gather accusations against Him. By the way, when you talk to others, do they draw near to hear more of what you have to say? Keep speaking the truth in love, and you will see that happen over and over again in your life.

Jesus is giving these sinners hope. Everyone needs hope. Whether it's a prisoner behind bars or the richest man on Wall Street, we all reach the point where we need hope. Jesus is truly the only hope Giver in this universe. Do people come to you because they see in you the hope they are looking for? And do they also know you will point them to Jesus as that hope Giver?

It is interesting to think about why sinners didn't draw near to the Pharisees for hope. Were these leaders not preaching

Jesus is truly the only hope Giver in this universe.

the teachings of the prophets in the Old Testament? Did people see no hope with these religious men? Are cults, gangs, and other groups growing exponentially because they are offering their members hope, even though it is a false hope? Is Islam growing because they offer men the false hope of 72 virgins and all the wine they want for eternity, even though it is all one big lie? People need hope, and the only foundation for real hope is truth.

Don't forget that the hearts of these sinners were tender. If they were drawing near to Jesus, they were drawing near to find truth. They had reached the point where they were searching for answers. Seekers have always been my favorite people to chat with.

The contrast between the coldness of the Pharisees and the loving heart of Jesus was obvious. It's easy to figure out which direction sinners would migrate. I was witnessing one day at the University of Southern California. One student told me I was the fourth person in two years to talk to him about Jesus. Devin explained how he really didn't enjoy his first three encounters because he felt like those folks had an agenda. He said, "I have really enjoyed this conversation, but thanks for not forcing anything on me." We don't need to force truth on people; we just need to share it with a loving heart.

THE UNTOUCHABLES

The Pharisees and Scribes made themselves untouchable. They placed themselves above the *basket of deplorables* whom they considered to be unredeemable sinners. They failed to realize that they were in the exact same boat as the ones they looked down upon. They needed a Savior just as much as everyone else. They should have been drawing near to Jesus, like the tax collectors and heathens were doing, but most of them refused.

> But go ye and learn what *that* meaneth, I will have mercy, and not sacrifice: for I am not come to call the righteous, but sinners to repentance. **Matthew 9:13**

It seems that these leaders were creating their own distinctions between the unclean and the righteous. They were sizing up others by outward appearances. How do you look at others when you see them? When someone is all tattooed or pierced up, what is your first thought? When you see someone in a three-piece suit, what runs through your mind? When you see someone tooling around in a beautiful convertible, what pops into your head?

If you saw a Rolls Royce convertible with a white person driving it, what would you be thinking? What if a Middle Eastern, Asian, or Hispanic person were behind the wheel? Let's get a little more personal. If you saw a black person in a totally awesome automobile, would you think he was a drug dealer, rap artist, professional athlete, successful businessman, or that his parents had a lot of money? Be very careful. Society can condition you to think in certain ways, and you may not be aware of the influence it exerts on you.

We were witnessing and handing out tracts at a Rolling Stones concert by the Georgia Tech football stadium one time. I was standing near a corner with a stoplight. All of a sudden, a Rolls Royce convertible pulled up! I happen to like that car, but I just don't see one in the driveway every day! The driver was a well dressed, black gentleman who was listening to some very loud music. My first thought was, *I bet he is a successful businessman here in Atlanta.* When I walked over to his car, he turned the music down. I said, "This is a beautiful car. I would like to ask you a question: If you died tonight, are you 100 percent assured that you would go to Heaven?" He stared at me, reached back

toward his radio, and turned the volume up extremely high. He had some really nice speakers in his ride! It was an impressive car that he will leave to someone else when he passes away. I wanted to see him in Heaven, so I did something about it.

"If you died tonight, are you 100 percent assured that you would go to Heaven?"

Another time, I was getting my rental car at the Baltimore airport. As I went to drive out and leave, there was one lane with three cars in it and one lane with no one in it. Well, that was an easy decision to make! I pray for the people I meet during my travels, and I also pray to go to the right checkout booths to meet the right people there, too.

As I drove up, Avery greeted me, and I said, "If you didn't have those big spikes there, it would be much easier to steal this car!" She looked at me and said, "We have much bigger problems than stealing in this world." So I asked, "What would one of those be?" She answered, "Racism." After hearing that, I knew we were going to have a good conversation!

I don't back away from discussions like these. Yes, they can be a little controversial at times. Yes, emotions can run a little hot. But these are also the times when truth can be put on the table to get people thinking.

I said to her, "I would have said *thou shalt not steal* is a much bigger problem than racism in our country. Okay, why do you say that?"

She shared some stories with me that definitely had the undertone of racism to them. She recounted one incident that would not have been a fun experience to go through at all.

So I looked at Avery and said, "Do you remember as a kid when you would come down the stairs on Christmas morning and turn the corner and see the tree, the ornaments, and the presents? Didn't you like it when they were all the exact same color?"

She got this really odd look on her face. She said, "No." I said, "No." Then I continued, "What we loved on Christmas morn was turning the corner and seeing the wide array and explosion of colors from all across the spectrum. Our eyes just soaked up all of those colors on that morning, yet when God wraps people in different colored packages, we seem to get all bent out of shape over it."

She looked at me humbly and responded, "That is the best analogy I have ever heard in my life."

So as we chatted about Christ (no cars came in my lane!!), I gave her some literature to read and a nice tip. I then looked at her and said, "Avery, never forget that the Bible says you are made in the image of God.

"The Bible says, Avery, that you were knit together, piece by piece, in your mother's womb.

"And did you know that the Bible says you are fearfully and wonderfully made in the eyes of Almighty God?

"And, Avery, if anyone ever tells you anything different, they are 100 percent wrong, and don't you ever forget that."

She looked at me sincerely and said, "Thank you." I reached over, shook her hand, and drove off to enjoy some time in the Baltimore traffic!

I will never forget Avery nor that look on her face at the end of our conversation. Just another one of those divine appointments that God has for us as we go through life.

By the way, how do you see yourself? As a creation of the Most High God? As a sinner in need of redemption, or as someone who needs no redemption? Would you put yourself in the unclean category or in the righteous category? Do you put people in different categories? Is there a section of people you look down on? Maybe the homeless? How about the less educated or the poor people in your town? What about people who live in the 'hood versus those who live in the high-society areas of your city? How about someone of a different race, homosexuals, or prisoners? Be careful. People are people. Humans are humans to Jesus. We all need the Savior. All.

By the way, how do you see yourself? As a creation of the Most High God? As a sinner in need of redemption, or as someone who needs no redemption?

However, the Pharisees murmured and complained about accepting sinners. They grumbled and criticized them. Their true heart was showing. Don't be like that yourself. You never want to be a murmurer or a complainer. Be a thankful person. Be a grateful person. Those kinds of people are always the most fun to hang out with in life.

> If we say that we have no sin, we deceive ourselves, and the truth is not in us. **1 John 1:8**

> Two men went up into the temple to pray; the one a Pharisee, and the other a publican. The Pharisee stood and prayed thus with himself, God, I thank thee, that I am not as other men *are*, extortioners, unjust, adulterers, or even as this publican. I fast twice

in the week, I give tithes of all that I possess. And the publican, standing afar off, would not lift up so much as *his* eyes unto heaven, but smote upon his breast, saying, God be merciful to me a sinner. I tell you, this man went down to his house justified *rather* than the other: for every one that exalteth himself shall be abased; and he that humbleth himself shall be exalted.   **Luke 18:10-14**

Now an interesting note to all of this is that these religious teachers, or professors, didn't realize they would be held to a stricter judgment. They knew the Scriptures. They should have been convicted over their sins, rather than judge others and discriminate against them. The arrogance and pride of these religious leaders had taken over, and they didn't understand the heart of God. That is a very bad place to be in life. The Pharisees murmured because Jesus held His arms wide open for the downtrodden, and they did not. They looked down on them, and Jesus did not. The people with leprosy and "AIDS" were just as important to Jesus as the kings and leaders. There is no caste system with Jesus, and there shouldn't be one with you either.

Jesus also sat down and spent time eating with sinners. There is something about having a meal with others. You learn a lot about them by listening to them, watching their mannerisms, and noticing how they interact with others. You also see who takes the last roll! One good thing to do with a lost person is take them out for a meal. I do that all the time. It is fun. It creates friendship. And it takes the pressure off of them because everyone eats. Everyone is used to sitting at a table with others. So many times, I don't even have to ask the first spiritual question because they will bring it up themselves.

How about you? Would you look down on someone so much that you would not sit down with them and give them the Word of God? Would you look up to some athlete or celebrity so much that you would not give them the Word of God? We want to be open and available to give out truth to all kinds of lost people.

SHEPHERDS SEEK

The true Shepherd cares about the whole flock. It is a large flock, made up of both Jews and Gentiles, but every one of them is precious to Him. The Shepherd doesn't want a single sheep to go astray. He cares about each and every one of them. If one does wander off, He will go find that sheep and bring it back to the flock. Think about that for a second. Who do you know today that might be wandering away from God? Are you doing something to go and get that person and bring them back to the Lord? Do you continue to reach out to those who don't return a single phone call, a single letter, or a single text message of yours? Are they that valuable to you? Never forget how valuable they are to God.

Who do you know today that might be wandering away from God? Are you doing something to go and get that person and bring them back to the Lord?

"No creature strays more easily than a sheep; none is more heedless; and none so incapable of finding its way back to the flock, when once gone astray: it will bleat for the flock, and still run on in an opposite direction to the place where the flock is: this I have often noticed. No creature is more defenceless than a sheep, and more exposed to be devoured by dogs and wild beasts. Even the fowls of the air seek their destruction. I have known ravens often attempt to destroy lambs by picking out their eyes, in which, when they have succeeded, as the creature does not see whither it is going, it soon falls an easy prey to its destroyer. Satan is ever going about as a roaring lion seeking whom he may devour; in order to succeed, he blinds the understanding of sinners, and then finds it an easy matter to tumble them into the pit of perdition. Who but a Pharisee or a devil would find fault with the shepherd who endeavors to rescue his sheep from so much danger and ruin!"[32]

To be honest, though, who is really more wayward than a human being? Sometimes, I think we make sheep look like the most obedient creatures on planet Earth! The lust of the eyes, the lust of the flesh, and the pride of life can take any one of us off the straight path. We can walk into the wilderness of sin without knowing there is a dead end or cliff up ahead, but we keep on walking, even when we know better. Is there any area of your life where you need to do a U-turn and return to the flock of believers and walk with them on the narrow road?

What if you went to school with one hundred people and one of them disappeared, but no one knew where he went. Would you send out a search party? Would you get on your four-wheeler and go find him? Or would you just sit back and wait to see if a storm blew him up on your front porch? Maybe you would say, *Ah, he is just one sheep. I still have ninety-nine others. No big deal. I am sure the wolves will enjoy their dinner tonight.* Or would you say, *Fellas, you watch these ninety-nine sheep. Don't let them go anywhere. I will be back soon.* Do you have compassion for the ones who have wandered off, or has this all just become a game of going through the motions to you?

"You would go in search of the lost directly. Turning your back upon the ninety and nine, and turning your thoughts from them too, you would leave them in their mountain pasture, as you sought the lost one. Calling it by its name, you would climb the terraced hills, and awake the echoes of the wadies, until the flinty heart of the mountain had felt the sympathy of your sorrow, repeating with you the lost wanderer's name. And when at last you found it, you would not chide or punish it; you would not even force it to retrace its steps across the weary distance, but taking compassion on its weakness, you would lift it upon your shoulders and bear it rejoicing home. Then forgetful of your own weariness, fatigue and anxiety swallowed up in the new-found joy, you would go round to your neighbors, to break the good news to them, and so all would rejoice together."[33]

> But when he saw the multitudes, he was moved with compassion on them, because they fainted, and were scattered abroad, as sheep having no shepherd. **Matthew 9:36**

I really can't wait to meet Jesus. I know one thing for sure that when I do, I am going to finally understand the mercy, love, and compassion that just ooze out of His being. It is who He is. Jesus cannot not have mercy. He cannot not have love. He cannot not have compassion. I need to exemplify His character so much better than I do now because soon I will meet the Author of mercy, love, and compassion and understand how these qualities were really supposed to have been lived out.

> For the Son of man is come to seek and to save that which was lost. **Luke 19:10**

What if Jesus leaving Heaven to come to Earth is being inferred in this passage? What if everything is just fine in the heavenlies, but Earth is a total mess? What if it is time for Him to show His creation the love and compassion He has for them? What if it is time for Him to go down to Earth and find those wandering sheep, and see if they want to come home?

> As a shepherd seeketh out his flock in the day that he is among his sheep *that are* scattered; so will I seek out my sheep, and will deliver them out of all places where they have been scattered in the cloudy and dark day. **Ezekiel 34:12**

The Shepherd left Heaven to seek and to save the lost. He actively came to seek out and save the wandering sheep Himself. This means we don't sit and wait for someone who is lost to come and knock on our door to hear the gospel; we go out to the highways and byways to seek for them. You can find lost people to talk with and hand out gospel tracts at places like: Art Festivals, Bar Sections of Town, Carnivals, Circuses, Community Events, Concerts, Craft Shows, Music Festivals, Sporting Events, State and County Fairs, Tailgating, Coffee Shops, Conferences, Farmers' Markets, Flea Markets, Laundromats, Malls, Public Sidewalks, Workplaces, City Parks, Holiday Celebrations, Parades, Abortion Clinics, Colleges, Schools, Airports, Bus Benches, Bus Stations, National Parks, Ski Resorts, Tourist Attractions, Vacation Sites, Boardwalks, and Beaches.

Imagine a sheep that is lost and cannot find its way back to the flock. It is floundering. It is now very vulnerable to predators. The beasts that prey on sheep are stirred. They have a meal in their sights. The remaining hours for this sheep are numbered. The shepherd has a different focus, though. He is urgently searching for his wayward sheep. The

How far would you go to find a lost sheep that might not make it through the night? Would you risk your life to find it?

lost sheep is far too important for him to give up on. He is on a rescue mission. All one hundred sheep in his flock are valuable to him: not just the ninety-nine.

The shepherd didn't send one of his children or a servant; he went himself. God did the same. How far would you go to find a lost sheep that might not make it through the night? Would you risk your life to find it?

> I am the good shepherd: the good shepherd giveth his life for the sheep.   **John 10:11**

God came Himself to die on the cross for the sins of the whole world. He is the Good Shepherd who said He would lay down His life for the sheep, and that is exactly what He did! What love!

> And I, if I be lifted up from the earth, will draw all *men* unto me.
> **John 12:32**

The Shepherd is drawing all people back to Himself and back into the fold. Make sure you heed His call.

We receive eight to ten letters a week from prisoners all across America who are reading our books in prisons and jails. We have decided that we want to reach these men and women for the Lord. They have strayed and gone wayward, and we want them to come to the saving knowledge of Jesus Christ. One of my friends used to go to church as a kid. He decided that fame, fortune, and the world were more important. So every year on his birthday or on Father's Day, I write him a card or a letter. Just reaching out to him one more time. It has been many years since he has responded. That is okay. That lost sheep is very important to me, but he is much more important to God.

LOST AND FOUND

When the shepherd finds his lost sheep, he is relieved. It has been running aimlessly in the wrong direction and is tired, worn out, and scared. But the shepherd has been tirelessly and relentlessly searching for it everywhere. Now that he has found his wayward sheep, he hoists it up to the safety and security of his shoulders. The shepherd has found his long lost sheep, and he is taking it home where it belongs.

As the shepherd carries his sheep back to the fold, he sustains and cares for it. The Lord Jesus Christ will sustain us, as well, no matter what trial we face. He cares for you, and He is completely faithful! So remember that when we are weak, He is strong! God is our strength. He can lift us up and carry us through those down times. Matter of fact, He loves doing just that!

For when we were yet without strength, in due time Christ died for the ungodly. **Romans 5:6**

Who his own self bare our sins in his own body on the tree, that we, being dead to sins, should live unto righteousness: by whose stripes ye were healed. For ye were as sheep going astray; but are now returned unto the Shepherd and Bishop of your souls.

1 Peter 2:24,25

All of the sins of the world have been laid upon His shoulders. Jesus not only died for your sins, but He died for the sins of every single person who has ever or will ever live. He died for the sins of the entire world! Forgiveness is available to all men.

And he is the propitiation for our sins: and not for ours only, but also for *the sins of* the whole world. **1 John 2:2**

Jesus died for the sins of the entire world! Forgiveness is available to all men.

All we like sheep have gone astray; we have turned every one to his own way; and the LORD hath laid on him the iniquity of us all.

Isaiah 53:6

As one guy has said, "Go in at the first 'all,' and come out at the last 'all'!" If we have all gone astray, then He has died for the sins of every person who has ever lived! What a Shepherd! What a Savior!

I have gone astray like a lost sheep; seek thy servant; for I do not forget thy commandments. **Psalm 119:176**

If you have gone astray, it is time to come back. If someone you know has gone astray, it is time to compel them to return to the loving arms of the Shepherd.

BURSTING WITH JOY

When a shepherd finds his lost sheep, he is excited! He rejoices! He tells his friends and family all about his lost sheep that is found!

And when he cometh home, he calleth together *his* friends and neighbours, saying unto them, Rejoice with me; for I have found my sheep which was lost. **Luke 15:6**

When do we rejoice in life? When do we throw a party? Celebrating the salvation of a lost sinner is reason for the angels and the Shepherd of the sheep to celebrate, and we should celebrate as well!

> Looking unto Jesus the author and finisher of *our* faith; who for the joy that was set before him endured the cross, despising the shame, and is set down at the right hand of the throne of God.
>
> **Hebrews 12:2**

Jesus suffered one of the most gruesome deaths known to mankind, yet He faced it with joy. Why? He knew the end result. He knew there would be multitudes upon multitudes of people who would be united with Him and His Father in Heaven. All the shame and all the suffering for the sins of others was worth it because many would be justified and saved.

> He shall see of the travail of his soul, *and* shall be satisfied: by his knowledge shall my righteous servant justify many; for he shall bear their iniquities.
>
> **Isaiah 53:11**

There is a satisfaction when you do your job correctly or accomplish the task that is in front of you. Jesus was one satisfied Savior on that cross! His sacrifice satisfied His Father and made salvation possible for the world. Never let that escape your thoughts.

You don't just share your troubles with your friends and neighbors, you share your joys as well! You don't have a baby and then not tell anyone. You shout it from the rooftops. You have great news to share. Your baby is alive and ready to begin the journey through planet Earth! And as parents, you are ready to nurture and train up your child to be a soldier for the King! Everyone has reason to rejoice!

If you think about it, the Pharisees should have been joyous when they saw the tax collectors and sinners drawing near to Jesus. These sinners were finally seeing the error of their ways. The religious people should have been excited, but they were not.

REPENTANCE

Not everyone wants to talk about repentance these days, but the Lord talked about it a lot. In fact, He repeated it three times in Luke 15, two of which are in our chapter's passage. The third mention is found a few verses later where Jesus says there is joy in Heaven when sinners repent.

> Likewise, I say unto you, there is joy in the presence of the angels of God over one sinner that repenteth. **Luke 15:10**

One guy that I really like to read is David Cloud, founder of Way of Life Literature at www.wayoflife.org. He once said, "Salvation is not difficult. It means to come to Jesus, but when you turn to Jesus, you have your back to the old life. That is repentance. It is like a man and marriage. When he receives one woman as his spouse, he has his back to all other women. Jesus taught that it is impossible to have two masters (Matthew 6:24). You cannot have Christ and the world."[34]

You see, this is the true heart of Jesus. He wants people to repent and believe in what He has done for them on the cross. True followers of our Lord should have the same heart. We should want to seek and to save those who are lost. We should be excited when someone expresses true biblical repentance and puts true biblical faith in the Lord Jesus Christ.

> I came not to call the righteous, but sinners to repentance. **Luke 5:32**

In verse 7 of our chapter's passage, there is a hint of irony when Jesus mentions the ninety-nine *just* people who need no repentance. Jesus knows everyone needs to repent and believe. He knows they all need forgiveness. But certain righteous people, like the Scribes and Pharisees, didn't think they needed repentance. They thought they were already righteous. I have heard people say they haven't asked God for forgiveness because they didn't think they needed to be forgiven of anything! Think about that for a second. Isn't that the crux of the problem? We either trust in ourselves and good works to get to Heaven, or we realize our sin and place our trust in God's great sacrifice on the cross for salvation. One or the other. That's the choice.

Sadly, the Pharisees trusted in themselves. They needed repentance but did not seek it or want it. You never, ever want to reach that point in your life.

"Repentance results in a change of life."

I was reading something else by David Cloud about repentance and thought he summed it up well: "In Acts 26:13-20, the Apostle Paul recounted the ministry that Christ had given to him by revelation. He was sent to the Gentiles 'to open their eyes, and to turn them from darkness to light, and from the power of Satan unto God' by exhorting them 'that they should repent and turn to God, and do works meet for repentance' (Acts 26:18,20). Consider three lessons from this. First, repentance was at the very heart of Paul's ministry. His objective was not to get men merely to 'believe' in Christ in a shallow sense, not just to get them to pray a 'sinner's prayer,' but to have them experience a radical turning… Second, we see that repentance must issue in faith (Acts 26:18). Repentance alone does not save; it must be accompanied by faith. In Acts 20:21, Paul described salvation as 'repentance toward God, and faith toward our Lord Jesus Christ.' Third, repentance results in a change of life (Acts 26:20). Paul preached the same thing as John the Baptist in the matter of repentance (Matthew 3:8). Some preachers today call this doctrine of repentance a 'lordship' or even a works salvation, but that is a slander. How can it be wrong to follow Paul's doctrine of repentance? Those who don't like it need to examine their own faith and trade their man-made 'quick prayerism' tradition for the pure Word of God. Biblical repentance is not works. It is not a change of life; it is a dramatic change of mind toward God that results in a change of life."[35]

As I was writing this section of the book, I got an email from a friend who wrote, "Because you know deep down that I am a good soul...I may not meet all your prerequisites, but at the end of the day, you know I'm a good person." Wow! How interesting is that?! The "prerequisites" I shared with him came from God's Word. They weren't standards that I set up. I let him know they were God's standards. The good thing is that he likes our give and take. He knows I care about him. And we will keep this communication going until he repents and believes or until he takes his last breath.

"Biblical repentance is not works. It is not a change of life; it is a dramatic change of mind toward God that results in a change of life."

The ones that Jesus refers to as "just persons" are probably those who consider themselves to be good. They could be those who see themselves as already righteous. They were brought up correctly and don't sin as often as others. They are not out drinking and carousing. They are not stealing from their employer. They are not trying to cheat someone in a business deal. They are upright citizens. They are not living in the ways of the world. They are not, in essence, a heathen like some other folks. They do not repent of their sins because they do not think sin is a part of their lives. Now, don't get me wrong, people like that are still not saved. They have still broken the Ten Commandments. Breaking one of them is the same as breaking all of them. They just are not the dirty, nasty sinners we tend to think of when we talk about someone who has strayed far from the narrow path.

For example, the disciples may have seemed outwardly good, but they all sinned and needed to repent. However, one of them actually sold Jesus Christ for thirty pieces of silver and never repented. That disciple sold one of his best friends for chump change. How could he do that? It was wicked to hand the Son of God over to death after knowing who He was and after watching Him do all of those miracles. All of the disciples had sinned, but Judas revealed he was in a totally different category.

WANDERING SHEEP

Sometimes when something is lost, you reach that point of despair. There is no hope left. That lost object will not be found. But do you remember that feeling of relief when you finally found what you had lost? By the way, what could be more important to God than the salvation of lost souls?

> My people hath been lost sheep: their shepherds have caused them to go astray, they have turned them away *on* the mountains: they have gone from mountain to hill, they have forgotten their restingplace. All that found them have devoured them: and their adversaries said, We offend not, because they have sinned against the Lord, the habitation of justice, even the Lord, the hope of their fathers. **Jeremiah 50:6,7**

> And the word of the Lord came unto me, saying, Son of man, prophesy against the shepherds of Israel, prophesy, and say unto them, Thus saith the Lord God unto the shepherds; Woe *be* to the shepherds of Israel that do feed themselves! should not the shepherds feed the flocks? Ye eat the fat, and ye clothe you with the wool, ye kill them that are fed: but ye feed not the flock. The diseased have ye not strengthened, neither have ye healed that which was sick, neither have ye bound up *that which was* broken, neither have ye brought again that which was driven away, neither have ye sought that which was lost; but with force and with cruelty have ye ruled them. And they were scattered, because *there is* no shepherd: and they became meat to all the beasts of the field, when they were scattered. My sheep wandered through all the mountains, and upon every high hill: yea, my flock was scattered upon all the face of the earth, and none did search or seek *after them*. **Ezekiel 34:1-6**

We live in troubled times. Shepherds are not doing what they are supposed to be doing. They should be preaching truth

and calling the lost to repentance and faith. They should be equipping the sheep to do the same. But instead, the sheep have been scattered. They have gone astray. The sheep have been wandering. They have been enticed by the entertainments and cares of the world.

"When asked by a Sydney Morning Herald reporter why the church is so successful, Brian Houston replied, 'We are scratching people where they are itching.' ("The Lord's Profits," Sydney Morning Herald, January 30, 2003). That is right out of 2 Timothy 4:3, which is a warning of apostasy. It describes people who itch for a new kind of Christianity, and it describes heaps of preachers who will scratch this illicit itch. 'For the time will come when they will not endure sound doctrine; but after their own lusts shall they heap to themselves teachers, having itching ears.'"[36]

Perhaps, like the Pharisees, shepherds have lost their way, too.

Brian Houston of Hillsong Church in Australia, who has campuses around the world, is so wrong here. Pastors are not supposed to scratch people where they itch. We don't conform our messages to please the people of the world. We don't give light and fluffy sermons so people will keep tithing. We speak truth. We do it in love. We speak and write books to glorify the Lord. That is it. Nothing else. Lost sheep need truth of the eternal kind today.

Where are the shepherds who will stand up for truth? Who will bring the wandering sheep back to the arms of their Savior? Who will teach them to walk on the road of faith? Who will instruct them to make spiritual sacrifices that please the heart of the Lord? Perhaps, like the Pharisees, shepherds have lost their way, too. Encourage your pastor to be on the narrow road. But even if everyone you know wanders in the days to come, that will not be you. You are focused on the Throne, pleasing the Lord, and knowing what matters for all of eternity.

Chapter 7
Group Discussion

1. How does the strength of our convictions and our love for others factor into the influence we have with them when giving out truth? Give an example of how someone listened to the gospel because they heard you speaking the truth in love.

2. Compare and contrast the welcoming attitude of Jesus toward sinners with the exclusive attitudes of the Pharisees. How does this mindset surface in some teachers today? Which displays the heart of God and why?

3. Is it possible for anyone to be excluded from Jesus' search for the lost? Who in Jesus' day excluded sinners from being found by God? What caused *them* to be excluded instead and why?

4. Why is it important to present the problem of sin to the lost when witnessing? What do the lost need to be saved from and why?

5. How did Jesus use the term *repentance* during His ministry on Earth? How have you heard *repentance* defined, and is that definition in agreement with the Bible?

6. Give some examples of people you know who refuse to believe they are a sinner. How does this affect their ability to come to Christ for forgiveness? What have they been unwilling to do?

7. Is there anyone that you have been afraid to share the gospel with or someone that you have avoided giving the gospel? How can you take steps to walk in their direction and trust God so you can boldly give them truth today?

8. List some of the places in your town where the lost gather and can be reached for Christ. What preparations can you make ahead of time, and what materials can you take with you to witness to them?

9. Have you ever had someone come to Christ after spending years in prayer for them and after having many conversations with them? Describe how you or others rejoiced with them after their conversion.

10. Is there a lost person in your life who needs someone to search for them? Will they make it through their next day, week, month, or year without your intervention? Did anyone make it their goal to search for you when you were lost in sin?

Luke 12:57-59

Yea, and why even of yourselves
judge ye not what is right?

When thou goest with thine
adversary to the magistrate,
as *thou art* in the way,
give diligence that thou mayest
be delivered from him;
lest he hale thee to the judge,
and the judge deliver thee to the officer,
and the officer cast thee into prison.

I tell thee, thou shalt not depart thence,
till thou hast paid the very last mite.

CHAPTER 8
Are You Able to Pay the Price?

RIGHT JUDGMENT

Jesus tells us that making a right judgment is simple. His phrase, "even of yourselves," implies it is plain. He expects the people to make the right call about His identity because His miracles and teachings have made it evident.

In Jesus' day, the Jewish leaders were passing unrighteous judgments against those who preached truth. John the Baptist preached repentance, and they wanted nothing to do with him. Jesus preached truth, and they didn't want the people listening to Him either. Why? Were they worried about their own popularity? Were they worried about Jesus gaining a large following? Did they just want to maintain the status quo?

Making a right judgment can rock the boat with those around you. Staying quiet might lead to a peaceful coexistence, but Jesus did not come to bring peace. He came to bring truth! You don't want to be a person who compromises with error just to keep the peace. It would be a false peace anyway.

If you know what is right, why won't you also judge by what is right? Because you might have a hidden agenda. You are not being honest with yourself or with others. You are actually being a hypocrite. You know the right thing to do or say in a situation, and you will not do it. You are more concerned with yourself and your outward appearance than about the Lord or others. That is a dangerous place to be in life. You have set yourself up on a pedestal. You care too much about the opinion of others. God will knock you off of that pedestal one day. It is much easier to just step down from it now (since it is His pedestal anyway!) and start judging righteously.

God has given us eternal truth, which is His Word, and it has stood the test of time.

> Judge not according to the appearance, but judge righteous judgment. **John 7:24**

If you judge righteously, you will see that all of the tenets of Scripture are true. God has given us eternal truth, which is His Word, and it has stood the test of time. Dig into it, and see how the truths He gave—from Genesis to Revelation—are just as true today as when He declared them. Why is that? Because the righteous Judge can never judge unrighteously!

TROUBLING TIMES

The Scriptures tell us that right and wrong do exist. Our duty is to do what is right, and it is not too difficult to discern. For example, look at the issue of transgendered people and using bathrooms. Just because someone is confused, doesn't mean we give up our common sense. Many who have had sex-change surgery want to change back. They have big regrets. They may change their looks on the outside, but their chromosomes stay the same on the inside.

Figuring out which bathroom to use should be a pretty simple matter, if you think about it. God has given each of us a certain kind of plumbing. Guys go to one bathroom and ladies go to another. You see, bathrooms are supposed to be biological and not social. But, of course, there is much more to this agenda than meets the eye. This is the breakdown of the family. This is an assault on what God says is right and wrong. God says man and woman in marriage, and the world says any combination of genders in marriage is fine. The Bible says to have kids within a heterosexual family, and the world says to have kids within any kind of family structure you want.

On a recent plane flight, a guy named John was sitting next to me. He loved logic. Everything had to be logical for him. When I asked him, "If you could have any job on planet Earth and money wasn't an issue, what would you want to do?" He didn't hesitate. He said, "Philosophy professor at a university!" I already knew this was going to be a good conversation, but his reply was icing on the cake!

Then out of nowhere he asked me, "What do you think about gay marriage?" This seems to be the only question on people's minds these days! Some people are interested in your answer; others just want to label you a bigot. Whether or not they want to categorize you doesn't matter; our job is to tell people the truth.

So I asked him, "When people get married, how many people get married?"

He responded that he didn't understand my question. So I said, "When you go to a marriage ceremony in India, China, Russia, Canada, or the United States, how many people are in that ceremony?"

He replied, "Two."

I then continued, "Where did the number come from?"

You should have seen the look on his face. He didn't have a clue. I let him know it came from the oldest writing ever on

the subject of marriage. It came from the Jewish Torah, and in the book of Genesis, it says:

> Therefore shall a man leave his father and his mother, and shall cleave unto his wife: and they shall be one flesh. **Genesis 2:24**

The interesting thing was that John knew the verse! When I said it out loud, he finished it by saying, "one flesh." Someone had taught him that verse at some point through the years. Then I said, "Whoever gets to tell you how many people can get married can also tell you who gets to be in that number." He loved the logic. But, of course, God is logical. That is why it is logical to believe in Him. I also read somewhere: *Whoever designs marriage gets to define marriage!* That is a good statement, and I have been using it as I talk with people about this subject.

Remember to keep pointing people to the Bible. It has all the answers that everyone needs.

Remember to keep pointing people to the Bible. It has all the answers that everyone needs regardless of how often it is denigrated in our society or literally destroyed in some of the classrooms around America. Never forget that the Word of God is indestructible because it is eternal.

So are you just going to roll over to the LGBT agenda, or are you going to stand and fight against what you know to be wrong? What will you do when their four-letter acronym becomes eight or ten letters? We need more soldiers on the front line now—not a year from now or a decade from now—*NOW!*

In today's world, Jesus would have run afoul of the political correctness police. Can you believe He had twelve disciples who were all men? What a bigot! Didn't He know He should have included women, gays, and transgenders among them? And I do hope those disciples weren't all men of the same color! If so, He would never have been able to preach on any college campus here in America. He would have been *persona non grata*.

Bear in mind that many people are being used as tools of Satan, and they don't even know it. Our job is to expose the deeds of darkness by shinning the light of truth on them.

> And have no fellowship with the unfruitful works of darkness, but rather reprove *them*.
> **Ephesians 5:11**

Our job is to expose the deeds of darkness by shinning the light of truth on them.

But one problem we have today is that many people do not believe in moral absolutes. They believe moral truth can be adjusted depending on the circumstance. Well, here is some simple advice: that is a recipe for disaster—disaster for people and for the culture we live in. The Bible either upholds these absolute truths, or it is just another book.

ACTING ON TRUTH

Judging correctly is critically important as we live this life. Christians need to be ready to stand before the Judgment Seat of Christ. We should also care deeply about the moment others stand before God, too. Meeting God will be a dreadful day for anyone who is not prepared.

> I have overthrown *some* of you, as God overthrew Sodom and Gomorrah, and ye were as a firebrand plucked out of the burning: yet have ye not returned unto me, saith the LORD. Therefore thus will I do unto thee, O Israel: *and* because I will do this unto thee, prepare to meet thy God, O Israel. For, lo, he that formeth the mountains, and createth the wind, and declareth unto man what *is* his thought, that maketh the morning darkness, and treadeth upon the high places of the earth, The LORD, The God of hosts, *is* his name.
> **Amos 4:11-13**

Many in Israel knew what was right, but they would not act on it. They had the knowledge of right and wrong, but they wouldn't put that knowledge into action. Think about that for a second. How many of us fall into the same category? We know the right thing to do, but we won't make the necessary stand because it might cost us something. But isn't standing for biblical truth worth whatever the cost? The days of not standing for righteousness need to end, and they need to end quickly.

Isn't standing for biblical truth worth whatever the cost?

And of the children of Issachar, *which were men* that had understanding of the times, to know what Israel ought to do.

1 Chronicles 12:32

Do you understand the times of our day? We are living in very troubling times. Lies are everywhere. Truth needs to return to the forefront, and you are the one to take it there.

I met a student at Brown University one time. He told me he didn't really grow up with any religious faith, but one of his goals in college was to find out what to believe in by the time he graduated! What a neat goal to have. I reminded him that he was not searching for something to believe in; he was searching for the truth. That really resonated with him, and we had a nice conversation about eternal truth.

RECONCILIATION

Notice that Paul says we are able to make proper judgments:

Dare any of you, having a matter against another, go to law before the unjust, and not before the saints? Do ye not know that the saints shall judge the world? and if the world shall be judged by you, are ye unworthy to judge the smallest matters? Know ye not that we shall judge angels? how much more things that pertain to this life? If then ye have judgments of things pertaining to this life, set them to judge who are least esteemed in the church. I speak to your shame. Is it so, that there is not a wise man among you? no, not one that shall be able to judge between his brethren?

1 Corinthians 6:1-5

You are responsible to judge righteously and to make the right call. It is up to you to perform the right actions to rectify the situation. If you have alienated someone for the wrong reason, make it right. If you have represented someone falsely, make it right. If you have wronged anyone in any way, make it right. It is the right thing to do.

And forgive us our debts, as we forgive our debtors. **Matthew 6:12**

Jesus is also teaching us to reconcile with others, even when they are our enemy. Someone who is against us. Someone who wants to destroy us, our family, or our church. If that is the case with our adversaries, then what should we do with a friend, acquaintance, or loved one whom we have wronged?

Reconcile with others before your door comes crashing down. Reconcile with God before consequences arrive on your doorstep.

Agree with thine adversary quickly, whiles thou art in the way with him; lest at any time the adversary deliver thee to the judge, and the judge deliver thee to the officer, and thou be cast into prison.

Matthew 5:25

After a courtroom verdict is reached, it is too late to make peace with your adversary. The judge tasks the officer or jailer with the responsibility to impose fines and sentences. He is someone to fear. He has the ability to cast you into prison. But judges always like to see people who are making progress in their community service hours and going to therapy. They can tell when someone is trying to make amends with their life and live the right way.

David Berkowitz, the Son of Sam serial killer who terrorized New York City back in the '70s, has repented of his sins and been saved! He actually runs the chapel in his prison. People who know him say that he has had a true born-again experience. If I have the story correct, he has been written up once since he has been in prison. That is it. And if you know anything about prison, that isn't a lot of write-ups. He was written up for giving a Bible to another inmate, which was considered contraband!

I have a friend who works as a chaplain in a prison where a murderer got saved. This prisoner had always been in trouble and was always put in solitary confinement. When I visited the prison six months after his salvation, he hadn't had one single write-up. He had been no trouble at all. Nice guy to be around. The guards kept asking the chaplain, "What happened to Kenneth?" They were hungry. They wanted to know. And it gave the chaplain the grand opportunity to share with these officers that it wasn't church, it wasn't religion, but it was Jesus Christ who changed Kenneth's life!

PEACE WITH YOUR ADVERSARY

When problems arise with an adversary, make restitution immediately. You don't want to wait for a lawsuit. Get it done. Prevent heartache for you and your family down the road. Do the right thing in the right way with the right attitude, and things will almost always work out.

Greed can get us into so much trouble. Taking advantage of people can ruin relationships. Make those things right. *NOW!* Better yet, don't walk into situations where people are being taken advantage of either in business or other relationships in the first place. No sense in causing them or yourself heartache.

Have a win-win attitude for everyone involved whenever problems come up. Have the mindset of, *I want to pay my debt, and you really don't want to go through the hassle of bringing me before the judge.* Or, *how can we find a solution and work this out?*

SETTLING OUT OF COURT

If you find yourself in a disagreement with an adversary that is severe enough to land you in court, you really want to settle matters before you reach the courtroom. Same with God: you want to settle your sin debt before you meet Him face to face. He is willing to settle out of court, which is why He graciously provided us with the perfect blood sacrifice of His Son on the cross. That blood will wash away *EVERY* transgression against Him, so you can meet Him in peace. Sounds like a great deal to take advantage of and a great deal to share with others.

> But if we walk in the light, as he is in the light, we have fellowship one with another, and the blood of Jesus Christ his Son cleanseth us from all sin. **1 John 1:7**

> And from Jesus Christ, *who is* the faithful witness, *and* the first begotten of the dead, and the prince of the kings of the earth. Unto him that loved us, and washed us from our sins in his own blood, **Revelation 1:5**

Shouldn't we make certain—beyond a shadow of a doubt—that we are ready for eternal judgment? Eternal judgment is serious business. It's nothing to play around with. It's something we need to take very, very seriously and implore others to take seriously as well.

Shouldn't we make certain—beyond a shadow of a doubt— that we are ready for eternal judgment?

> And many of them that sleep in the dust of the earth shall awake, some to everlasting life, and some to shame *and* everlasting contempt. **Daniel 12:2**

> But why dost thou judge thy brother? or why dost thou set at nought thy brother? for we shall all stand before the judgment seat of Christ. For it is written, *As* I live, saith the Lord, every knee shall bow to me, and every tongue shall confess to God. So then, every one of us shall give account of himself to God. **Romans 14:10-12**

And as it is appointed unto men once to die, but after this the judgment: **Hebrews 9:27**

And I saw a great white throne, and him that sat on it, from whose face the earth and the heaven fled away; and there was found no place for them. And I saw the dead, small and great, stand before God; and the books were opened: and another book was opened, which is *the book* of life: and the dead were judged out of those things which were written in the books, according to their works. And the sea gave up the dead which were in it; and death and hell delivered up the dead which were in them: and they were judged every man according to their works. And death and hell were cast into the lake of fire. This is the second death. And whosoever was not found written in the book of life was cast into the lake of fire.   **Revelation 20:11-15**

God's Law will be our ultimate judge. Unredeemed sinners will be found guilty before Almighty God on Judgment Day. That is very sobering to think about. Wrestle with the scenario of walking into a courtroom in your city and knowing that you will be found guilty before the trial even begins. What would your attitude be like during the trial? But what if you were told that you could be found not guilty before even setting foot in the courthouse? Would you take advantage of that proposition? Would you accept the plea bargain from the prosecutor to drop all charges? Likewise, will you take God's offer of mercy that He accomplished for you on the cross? Will you please tell others about that offer of mercy before they sit down at the defendant's table before the Judgment Seat of Christ?

Remember, your adversary has an advantage before an earthly judge. You are in debt to him—he knows it and you know it, and now the judge is going to know it. Just the same, our sin has put us in debt with God. Our sin has made us His enemy. We have offended Him, and we need to make peace.

Go, tell Jeroboam, Thus saith the LORD God of Israel, Forasmuch as I exalted thee from among the people, and made thee prince over my people Israel, And rent the kingdom away from the house of David, and gave it thee: and *yet* thou hast not been as my servant David, who kept my commandments, and who followed me with all his heart, to do *that* only *which was* right in mine eyes; But hast done evil above all that were before thee: for thou hast gone and made thee other gods, and molten images, to provoke me to anger, and hast cast me behind thy back: **1 Kings 14:7-9**

Rebelling against God and provoking Him to anger is not a good way to go through life. If we avoid making earthly adversaries because it makes life a mess, we do not ever want to have God as our adversary either. We don't want to cast Him behind our back. Get the slate clean with Him right away. Take your pardon while it is still available to you, because once you are found guilty and once you're in prison, you can't say, *Okay, now I am going to get right with the judge.* It is too late. Way, way too late. You needed to do that before you entered the courtroom of God. You must get right with the eternal Judge before you are brought before Him.

So are you living your life in the hands of the adversary or in the hands of the Father? This life is not to be wasted. It is to be lived fully for the Lord. As I tell people, "Get saved, tell everyone you possibly can about Jesus, take your last breath, get out of this crazy place, and go enjoy Jesus for all of eternity!" Now that is a life well lived!

WORTH EVERY PENNY

As I parked my car to take a walk one day, I noticed a nice, shiny penny glinting in the sun beside my vehicle. That penny might not have much value to us, but to someone who needs only one cent to pay off an entire bill, it is worth much more than it seems. Same with a mite. It may have been the least of all coins, but every mite was needed to pay off an outstanding debt.

I was reading about a lady whose home was sold out from under her by the government. She didn't pay her taxes on time, so the government sold her house to a group that would then sell it for a profit. She was about to be evicted from her home. She was an older lady. She would not budge. When it was all said and done, there had been a mistake in the paperwork, and she was three cents short of paying her taxes! They sold her home for that reason! Three of those small, shiny coins can go further than we might imagine.

Never forget that your sin debt to God can never be paid by you. There is literally nothing you can do to pay it off. You can't hand Him a penny or a million dollars for your sins. You can't hand Him church attendance, good deeds, an awesome Grade Report, or your Yard of the Month award. Any weeping or wailing over your sins will not remove them either. Nothing but the blood of Christ can wipe your sin debt clean.

Therefore thou art inexcusable, O man, whosoever thou art that judgest: for wherein thou judgest another, thou condemnest thyself; for thou that judgest doest the same things. But we are sure that the judgment of God is according to truth against them which commit such things. And thinkest thou this, O man, that judgest them which do such things, and doest the same, that thou shalt escape the judgment of God? Or despisest thou the riches of his goodness and forbearance and longsuffering; not knowing that the goodness of God leadeth thee to repentance? But after thy hardness and impenitent heart treasurest up unto thyself wrath against the day of wrath and revelation of the righteous judgment of God; Who will render to every man according to his deeds: To them who by patient continuance in well doing seek for glory and honour and immortality, eternal life: But unto them that are contentious, and do not obey the truth, but obey unrighteousness, indignation and wrath, Tribulation and anguish, upon every soul of man that doeth evil, of the Jew first, and also of the Gentile; But glory, honour, and peace, to every man that worketh good, to the Jew first, and also to the Gentile: For there is no respect of persons with God. **Romans 2:1-11**

God is no respecter of persons—never has been and never will be. We all must come to Him through the blood of Christ, or we will miss out on being with Him for all of eternity in Paradise. Be careful. Many people who reason otherwise think they've got it going on, but Judgment Day will sort all of that out. For many people, the last will be first and the first will be last.

> Even as the Son of man came not to be ministered unto, but to minister, and to give his life a ransom for many.   **Matthew 20:28**

> Who gave himself a ransom for all, to be testified in due time.   **1 Timothy 2:6**

No shiny pennies needed for eternity. The blood of Christ will do just fine! Maybe our best bet is to seek the Lord while He may still be found.

Time is a precious commodity. Use it very wisely in your life. It might be gone sooner than you think.

> For this shall every one that is godly pray unto thee in a time when thou mayest be found: surely in the floods of great waters they shall not come nigh unto him.
> **Psalm 32:6**

It seems like the floodwaters are rising all around us. There is so much sin, deception, and evil in the world. There is no telling how much time we have left. Noah preached for 120 years, and when the end came, so many people were not prepared to meet God. Our final days are fast approaching, too.

> Again, he limiteth a certain day, saying in David, To day, after so long a time; as it is said, To day if ye will hear his voice, harden not your hearts.   **Hebrews 4:7**

Time is a precious commodity. Use it very wisely in your life. It might be gone sooner than you think.

PAYING THE PRICE

When you have broken a law, you can't claim ignorance of the law. The law is the law. Citizens should keep updated about them. Now in our society, we pass too many laws to keep up with them all, but God has written His Law on our hearts. Our consciences tell us when we are guilty of wrongdoing.

> Which shew the work of the law written in their hearts, their conscience also bearing witness, and *their* thoughts the mean while accusing or else excusing one another;) **Romans 2:15**

"So we find that the plea of ignorance is a mere refuge of lies, and none can plead it who has the book of God within his reach, and lives in a country blessed with the preaching of the Gospel of Jesus Christ."[37]

Claiming ignorance as a defense before God won't work. People down here should be searching for answers and asking the questions: *What if there is a God? How did this world get here? Did God create it, or did it come into being by luck and by chance over time? Will He judge me? Am I good enough to be in His presence, or do I need forgiveness?*

Human effort is not the currency that can pay off your debt of sin.

People are heaping up a mountain of sin before the Lord. Are you helping them get ready for the day they will be called to account for that sin?

Others may be able to help you pay the mite that you owe to creditors, but they cannot help you pay the penalty you owe to God for the unrighteous sins you have committed during your lifetime. Human effort is not the currency that can pay off your debt of sin.

Imelda Marcos from the Philippines used to walk on her knees from the back of her Catholic church all the way to the front. She thought that her suffering would pay for her sins. When she meets Jesus, she will realize that she was deceived.

Muslims believe there is a great weighing scale that weighs their good deeds against their bad deeds to determine where they will spend eternity. Again, that won't be happening. So to avoid taking their chances with the weighing scale, they're taught that if they die as a martyr for Allah, they can skip judgment and go directly to Paradise! Nope. Their ticket must be stamped in the blood of Jesus Christ, or they will not be entering Paradise for all of eternity.

Jesus tells us in verse 59 of our chapter's passage that the guilty cannot pay their sin debt. They can't get that last penny. They don't have it, and no one can lend it to them or give it to them. Anyone who stands before the Lord without having their sins washed away by His blood will have no ability to pay off their eternal debt of sin.

Remember, there is a great penalty for not having your sin debt paid in full before you stand before the Judge.

> And these shall go away into everlasting punishment: but the righteous into life eternal. **Matthew 25:46**

> Who shall be punished with everlasting destruction from the presence of the Lord, and from the glory of his power; **2 Thessalonians 1:9**

> And the smoke of their torment ascendeth up for ever and ever: and they have no rest day nor night, who worship the beast and his image, and whosoever receiveth the mark of his name. **Revelation 14:11**

> Where their worm dieth not, and the fire is not quenched. **Mark 9:48**

> And shall come forth; they that have done good, unto the resurrection of life; and they that have done evil, unto the resurrection of damnation. **John 5:29**

Hell is eternal. Hell is painful. Hell is where there is weeping and gnashing of teeth. Hell is where the punishment for every lie, lust, and larceny will be paid. Even the smallest of sins needs to be rectified with Almighty God. Thank you, Jesus, for every drop of blood that washes away every impurity we have ever committed!

TIME IS RUNNING OUT

Time is of the essence. You don't know how much life you have left before death comes knocking on your door. You could be standing in front of God in an instant—quicker than you can imagine. You don't get a do-over when that day arrives. You don't get a mulligan. You don't get a second chance. Be sure you make peace with God before it is too late. Life. Death. Judgment Day. Make sure you are ready.

> And that, knowing the time, that now *it is* high time to awake out of sleep: for now *is* our salvation nearer than when we believed. The night is far spent, the day is at hand: let us therefore cast off the works of darkness, and let us put on the armour of light.
> **Romans 13:11,12**

> LORD, make me to know mine end, and the measure of my days, what it *is: that* I may know how frail I *am.* **Psalm 39:4**

> So teach *us* to number our days, that we may apply *our* hearts unto wisdom. **Psalm 90:12**

> Whereas ye know not what *shall be* on the morrow. For what *is* your life? It is even a vapour, that appeareth for a little time, and then vanisheth away. **James 4:14**

> And David sware moreover, and said, Thy father certainly knoweth that I have found grace in thine eyes; and he saith, Let not Jonathan know this, lest he be grieved: but truly as the LORD liveth, and as thy soul liveth, *there is* but a step between me and death. **1 Samuel 20:3**

> For all flesh *is* as grass, and all the glory of man as the flower of grass. The grass withereth, and the flower thereof falleth away: But the word of the Lord endureth for ever. And this is the word which by the gospel is preached unto you. **1 Peter 1:24,25**

> Man is like to vanity: his days *are* as a shadow that passeth away. **Psalm 144:4**

I drove up behind a truck the other day. It had a very big picture of a guy, and it said "In Memory Of..." So at the next stoplight, I pulled up alongside the guy. He rolled his window down. I said, "I saw the sticker for Patrick Brownlee on the back of your truck. Was he born again? Was he saved?" The man looked at me and said, "Yes" as tears came to his eyes.

Patrick was his twin brother. They were born three minutes apart. Patrick was forty-five years old when he died.

He told me through the open window that early in the morning on the day his brother died, he felt deep within his spirit that something just wasn't right. Then later that day, he got the call from his mom that his brother had died. When he found out the time of his brother's death, he realized it was the exact same moment when the feeling had come over him earlier that morning.

The clock is ticking toward the midnight hour. Your life is coming to a close. Are you ready to meet the King on Judgment Day?

I tossed a book to him through the open window and encouraged him; then the light turned green, and we parted ways.

The clock is ticking toward the midnight hour. Your life is coming to a close. Are you ready to meet the King on Judgment Day? Every person's life around you is coming to an end, too. The closing of the curtain is drawing nigh. There is no curtain call. There is no encore. You are not looking for the audience's applause. You want to hear, *Well done, My good and faithful servant* from Jesus and nothing else. Those around you have one life to live, and then they meet the King. Are you getting lost people ready for their encounter with the One True God?

> Lay not up for yourselves treasures upon earth, where moth and rust doth corrupt, and where thieves break through and steal: But lay up for yourselves treasures in heaven, where neither moth nor rust doth corrupt, and where thieves do not break through nor steal: For where your treasure is, there will your heart be also.
>
> **Matthew 6:19-21**

GET YOUR AFFAIRS IN ORDER

Keep in mind that you are just passing through this place called planet Earth. Be as wise in your eternal affairs with God as you are in your temporal affairs with men. We tend to make sure all is right in our relationships with men by investing time in business relationships and dotting every "i" and crossing every "t" in legal contracts. But do we realize that today we could meet the Son of Man who died on that cross? Please get your eternal affairs in order—*TODAY!*

None of us wants our house foreclosed on, so we pay our mortgage payment on time. If we get behind, we try to catch up. We might even get to the point where we cannot pay the mortgage. If that happens, we go to the bank and talk with our banker to see if there is any way we can restructure our loan debt so we or our family are not out on the streets. We work

hard to make sure our temporal affairs are in order, and we should work doubly hard to make sure our eternal affairs are in order as well.

The time is short. Be about the Lord's work now.

For God shall bring every work into judgment, with every secret thing, whether *it be* good, or whether *it be* evil. **Ecclesiastes 12:14**

Alarm bells are going off. Warning signals are flashing. Sirens are blaring. They are sounding all around us. The time is short. Be about the Lord's work now.

If we plead our own righteousness before God, we are in for an eternal world of hurt. If we bank on our own justification, we are in big trouble. He is the Righteous One, and we are not. We will be found guilty and cast into the prison of Hell where we must pay every last mite for all the sins we have committed.

If you end up in Hell, you will not get out until the last mite is paid. No one else can pay it; you must pay it. You must bring the judge remittance. But the catch is that you have no way to pay off your debt. And once your sentence begins, there is no way for the debt to be forgiven. That means your sentence will span throughout all of eternity with no hope of pardon, which should be a very sobering thought for all of us.

The time to make peace with God is before that eternal judgment takes place. You must be holy to stand before a holy God. You must be cleansed of sin His way. He has made it very simple, but since it is a narrow road, most people really want to do it their own way. That is their choice, but there is an eternal consequence for that choice.

> For *there is* one God, and one mediator between God and men, the man Christ Jesus; **1 Timothy 2:5**

> And all things are of God, who hath reconciled us to himself by Jesus Christ, and hath given to us the ministry of reconciliation; To wit, that God was in Christ, reconciling the world unto himself, not imputing their trespasses unto them; and hath committed unto us the word of reconciliation. **2 Corinthians 5:18,19**

God's arm is outstretched to take any sinner to Heaven who repents and trusts in this sacrifice.

> With a strong hand, and with a stretched out arm: for his mercy *endureth* for ever. **Psalm 136:12**

God has reconciled the world to Himself through the sacrifice of His Son. His arm is outstretched to take any sinner to Heaven who repents and trusts in this sacrifice. Will you take advantage of His offer of mercy? Don't hesitate. The time is now. Will you also extend this offer to many more people before they take their last breath? Will you help others to make the right decision about their sin, Jesus Christ, and the coming Judgment? Please take advantage of this great gift, and help others do the same before time runs out.

Chapter 8
Group Discussion

1. What kinds of judgments should Christians be making as they go through their days? Which judgment calls are right or wrong to make? Give reasons for your answers.

2. What provisions has God given to all people so they can discern right from wrong?

3. When we make right judgments in life, who are we pleasing and who are we protecting? What are some of the consequences for failing to make proper judgments?

4. What do we learn about God, His Word, and ourselves when we obey or disobey His commands?

5. How does keeping a right relationship with others also keep peace between you and the Lord?

6. What do we reveal about our attitude toward God and His forgiveness if we put His words to the side and sin?

7. When your better judgment warns you that sin or trouble is lurking in your path, what should be your response? Name some of the costs for ignoring those warnings and some of the benefits for heeding them.

8. When is it too late for a lost person to make peace with God? How precious does that make our time on Earth? What are some of the best ways to use our time in life?

9. Explain what things cannot be offered to God as payment for sins. How does this help answer the question of why eternal suffering never ends?

10. What payment for sin will God accept? Tell about a recent opportunity when you were able to explain the consequences and remedy for sin to a lost person.

John 8:45-51

And because I tell *you* the truth,
ye believe me not.

Which of you convinceth me of sin?
And if I say the truth, why do ye not believe me?

He that is of God heareth God's words:
ye therefore hear *them* not,
because ye are not of God.

Then answered the Jews, and said unto him,
Say we not well that thou art a Samaritan,
and hast a devil?

Jesus answered, I have not a devil;
but I honour my Father,
and ye do dishonour me.

And I seek not mine own glory:
there is one that seeketh and judgeth.

Verily, verily, I say unto you,
If a man keep my saying, he shall
never see death.

CHAPTER 9
Whose Honor Are You Seeking?

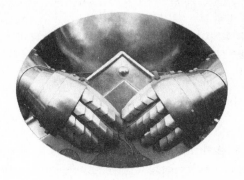

BLINDED BY SIN

Jesus came to Earth on a mission. He came to seek and to save lost souls. He knows they cannot be saved or be pleasing to His Father unless they know and believe the truth. Truth is the starting point of faith. And Jesus perfectly taught and displayed the truth of God with every word He spoke and with every deed He performed. Jesus was Truth in human flesh.

Earlier in John 8, Jesus pointed out to the Pharisees that His Father and their father are not one and the same.

> I speak that which I have seen with my Father: and ye do that which ye have seen with your father.   **John 8:38**

Jesus tried to simplify things for the people and for the Pharisees. They would believe and follow the devil, but they would not believe and follow Him. Just think about that for a second. Process that. It is fascinating to contemplate. One or the other—God or Satan—and yet, they chose to follow Satan.

Jesus is the only One who is telling them the truth. He is the Author of truth. Him alone. Not anyone else. This battle for truth was coming down to them versus Jesus, and they would not win. They couldn't put the blame for their unbelief anywhere else. They could heap everything they had at Jesus because He and His Father could handle it. So as you meander through the journey of life, Jesus—and Jesus alone—has the truth you are seeking.

> To the law and to the testimony: if they speak not according to this word, *it is* because *there is* no light in them. **Isaiah 8:20**

Even though the Pharisees did not believe in Him, they did believe in something. Everybody believes in something, but these religious leaders refused to believe in truth!

I was talking with a Jewish man this summer while I was out witnessing one day. I asked him if he believed that Jesus was the Messiah, or the *Mashiach*. He said, "I wish you wouldn't proselytize me!" I will never forget those words. Most people don't even know what the word *proselytize* means! It is his call to search for truth or not, but it is my job to give truth to him and to others when I talk with them.

While witnessing at UC Fullerton one day, I ran into Hector. It was easily one of the greatest conversations I have ever had. At age 23, he had studied Theosophy, Energy, Roman Catholicism, Evangelical Christianity, Hinduism, Atheism, and Rosicrucianism! I wondered when Hector ever slept! He told me that he literally thinks about death all the time! He loves to read, so I gave him a book that would help answer his questions. I emphatically told him that he was not looking for something to believe in; he was looking for truth—and nothing but the truth. And if he searched for it, he would find it. What an encounter. There are other people like Hector out there. Are you reaching them with the truths of the Bible and the cross of our Lord Jesus Christ?

Remember, your job isn't to tell people what they want to hear; your job is to tell them the truth. I always say, "If the truth hurts, it is still the truth!" People have been told enough lies in this crazy world. Let them wrestle with truth. It will be good for them in the long run.

When Jesus delivered eternal truth from the Father to the religious leaders—truth that has stood the test of time and will stand the test of eternal time—many of them believed Him not. If He had delivered lies to them, they would have invited Him over for a barbecue lunch after church. But His stomach was not more important to Him and His Father than truth. Jesus could have taken five loaves of bread and two fish and made a buffet for them whenever He felt like it. Eternal souls are always more important to Him than food. People might mock Him and laugh at Him, but truth spoken in love is what they would get from Him.

These leaders were so estranged from God that they didn't even recognize that they were standing next to eternal Truth. They loved the darkness rather than the light, even though the true Light was shining right at them. Their days would be coming to a screeching halt soon. The darkness would not prevail much longer.

PERFECTLY FAULTLESS

Jesus is divine, yet the Pharisees are trying to convict Him of sin! No matter how many false accusations they bring against Him, none of them will stick. His conscience is clear. There is nothing there to convict Him of, and there is nothing there for a reason—He is God. He is the spotless, sinless Savior. What could they say that would change that? Nothing. Jesus was tempted in all the same ways as we are, yet was without sin. What a Savior!

Since Jesus is free from sin, whenever He speaks, He speaks truth! Nothing but truth rolls across His lips into the world of lies around Him.

These Jews have watched Jesus up close and from a distance. They know they have no grounds to accuse Him. They might try and convict Him of sin, but their arsenal of weapons against Him is empty. They might throw darts at Him with certain sins written on them, but they will fall well short of hitting the King. They might put a bullseye on His back, but they will never hit Him. Jesus speaks truth; they speak lies. Jesus is not—and cannot ever be—in error in any way.

In verse 46 of our chapter's passage, there might have been a pause between the two questions that Jesus asked the Pharisees. He probably asked the first question, "Which of you convinceth me of sin?" and found that they were at a loss for words. Dead silence. So the next question, "And if I say the truth, why do ye not believe me?" naturally followed. He is showing them they have no logical reason to reject Him.

These leaders want to kill Jesus (John 7:1), yet Jesus is giving them the opportunity to reconsider their plot against Him. Of course, He knows, and they know, He is not guilty of sin and is not worthy of a death sentence. They have no justification to put Him to death because they would not, and would not ever, find any sin in Him.

> I have not written unto you because ye know not the truth, but because ye know it, and that no lie is of the truth.   **1 John 2:21**

In other words, they could give it their best shot. They could dig deep and research His entire life—talk to all of His friends, relatives, and enemies—and they would find nothing. His life was a clean slate. Matter of fact, it was a very clean slate—like empty clean! That is what holiness is, and that is how holiness lives.

Since Jesus has no sin, He has nothing to repent of and nothing that brings Him shame. The Scribes and Pharisees have plenty of both! They think that if they can find a flaw in this Man, they can discredit Him and His ministry. Now, sin cannot ever discredit truth. Truth is truth. It never, ever changes. But when a life is wrapped around truth and lived for the Lord, it is a deadly combination. Our words and actions should go hand in hand. If they haven't been walking together in your life, repent and get back on track.

NO EXCUSES

Jesus wants them to think about why they will not believe in Him. He wants their best reason—something that would hold water. It is their moment to make their case. This is a climatic point in history, and they are missing it. Jesus knows they really don't want to miss this moment. He knows that many others have realized eternal Truth was standing before them, so what are their reasons for not believing in Him, too?

> I have many things to say and to judge of you: but he that sent me is true; and I speak to the world those things which I have heard of him. **John 8:26**

> For he whom God hath sent speaketh the words of God: for God giveth not the Spirit by measure *unto him.* **John 3:34**

> For I have given unto them the words which thou gavest me; and they have received *them,* and have known surely that I came out from thee, and they have believed that thou didst send me. **John 17:8**

These verses show as clear as a bell—as clear as a window that has just been Windexed—that Jesus speaks the words of God. He speaks nothing less than pure truth. You are either heeding His words or rejecting His words. He leaves you no middle ground. Simple. The importance of knowing and believing His words is the difference between life and death. You can tell the difference. Your spirit knows it.

> We are of God: he that knoweth God heareth us; he that is not of God heareth not us. Hereby know we the spirit of truth, and the spirit of error. **1 John 4:6**

> Why do ye not understand my speech? *even* because ye cannot hear my word. Ye are of *your* father the devil, and the lusts of your father ye will do. He was a murderer from the beginning, and abode not in the truth, because there is no truth in him. When he speaketh a lie, he speaketh of his own: for he is a liar, and the father of it.
> **John 8:43,44**

These people can choose to believe that Jesus speaks the words of God, but they are following the wrong leader. They need to give up following their father the devil, repent, and turn toward the King. Then everything will become clear to them. Deciding to follow either the lusts of Satan or the love of God should be an easy choice, but to make the obviously right decision means they will have to admit they have been wrong. Never underestimate the reluctance of people—especially the male species—to admit they are wrong. Men, especially those in authority, hate to be wrong or admit they have been wrong. Will their stubbornness win out, or will humbleness rule the day?

"Rabbis and priests, teachers of the Law, judges of truth, offerers of sacrifice, keepers of feasts, worshippers in synagogues and Temple—they were all this; but they were not 'of God.'"[38]

Jesus is giving them hard truth because He wants them to believe. They can't hear that truth because they are rejecting *the* Truth. They have sided with evil and lies instead. Jesus wants them to leave their world of unbelief behind. He wants them to walk away from the evil one. He wants them to understand that the lust of the eyes, the lust of the flesh, and the pride of life cannot take them anywhere they want to go. The Holy Spirit is drawing them through truth. They have free will, and they need to use it to repent and believe. They need to come to Him before it is too late. *NOW* is always the appropriate time to believe!

> (For he saith, I have heard thee in a time accepted, and in the day of salvation have I succoured thee: behold, now *is* the accepted time; behold, now *is* the day of salvation.)
> **2 Corinthians 6:2**

CHAPTER 9

THE SAMARITAN SLUR

Undoubtedly, the term *Samaritan* is being used by the Pharisees in a derogatory way. The Samaritans were the hated neighbors of the Jews. By calling Jesus a Samaritan, the Jews are showing their utter disdain for Him. They are mocking Him. They are sneering at Him. Truth is piercing their hearts, and since they will not hear it or obey it, they attack the Messenger.

This slur was probably a customary insult of the Pharisees, meaning one of the things they would say to get under someone's skin. It irked the Pharisees that Jesus preached and lodged among the Samaritans. He received them. He performed miracles among them. And because Jesus hung out with these sinners, the Pharisees insinuated that He must be one, too.

> And one of them, when he saw that he was healed, turned back, and with a loud voice glorified God, And fell down on *his* face at his feet, giving him thanks: and he was a Samaritan. **Luke 17:15,16**

Out of the ten men whom Jesus cleansed of leprosy, only the Samaritan came back to thank Him. This verse, taken from Luke 17, shows us the humility of the Samaritans as compared with the arrogance of some of the Jews. And isn't it interesting that we also have a parable called *The Good Samaritan*? Again, the Samaritan showed the type of love that these Jewish leaders did not show at all. Calling Jesus a *Samaritan* could never have been a slur to Him because the Samaritans were more thankful and treated Him better than many of the Jews.

> Who, when he was reviled, reviled not again; when he suffered, he threatened not; but committed *himself* to him that judgeth righteously: **1 Peter 2:23**

Apparently, the charge of being a Samaritan didn't bother Jesus because He didn't answer their slur. He dismissed it. He knew these leaders were creations of the Most High God, so He let the insult slide. That might be some good advice for all of us.

> Then saith the woman of Samaria unto him, How is it that thou, being a Jew, askest drink of me, which am a woman of Samaria? for the Jews have no dealings with the Samaritans. **John 4:9**

The Scribes and the Pharisees were notorious for elevating themselves above the common people, yet they were getting their comeuppance from the One they wanted everyone to despise. Jesus desperately wants them to repent and believe, so He gives them unvarnished truth. Instead of seeing themselves in the right light, they opposed truth, called names, and made false accusations. Many of the Samaritans, whom these leaders rejected and hated, were the ones coming to Jesus for salvation! And many of these Samaritans might have been much more open to God than the Levites, Pharisees, or Rabbis!

> And many of the Samaritans of that city believed on him for the saying of the woman, which testified, He told me all that ever I did. **John 4:39**

Jesus' words should have softened the hearts of everyone who heard Him, including the Pharisees. Instead, these leaders were taking the wrong road. They were allowing their hearts to be hardened. Whenever anyone chooses that path, there is only a dead-end straight ahead of them.

NAME-CALLING

Since the Jews could find no sin in Jesus, they tried another approach to discredit Him; they resorted to name-calling! If the Jews could prove that Jesus had a demon, they could label Him a lunatic. Then no one would need to pay attention to Him again.

There might have been another reason why the Pharisees labeled Jesus *demon-possessed:* "The history of Simon Magus reminds us that the people of Samaria, from the least to the greatest, had been for a long time under the influence of his sorceries…it is probable that there is a special connection in the words here, 'Thou art a Samaritan, and hast a demon.'"[39]

When the Pharisees say *He must have a devil,* they were implying that He is completely different from them. The Jews think they are on God's side and that Jesus is on the other team. It's like they are saying, *We might be on the same playing field, but you are on the devil's team, and we serve the God of Abraham, Isaac, and Jacob.* The good news is they realize that Jesus is totally different in character from them. The bad news is they have the teams mixed up! They are actually wearing demonic uniforms with their own names stitched on the back, and they don't even know it.

> Woe unto them that call evil good, and good evil; that put darkness for light, and light for darkness; that put bitter for sweet, and sweet for bitter!
> **Isaiah 5:20**

Isn't it interesting that people in our culture can also serve Satan without realizing it? Look at the social causes that people stand up for and support. For instance, they often say that a woman has a right to choose. Always ask them, "To choose what?" To choose to murder a baby puts them on the devil's team, not on God's team.

Further, if you or someone else opposes the "socially accepted" sins of our culture, then you or they might be called a racist, bigot, homophobe, Islamophobe, Nazi, or intolerant. When others resort to name-calling, it typically means they don't have a valid argument.

As Christians, we have dealings with all kinds of people. We want everyone to be saved. We don't categorize others or refuse to hang out with certain groups. We never want to put ourselves in a high and mighty class because of the position we hold in life, our money, our smarts, or our athletic abilities. Be careful. God made everyone. All lives matter to God. He wants all of them to be reached for Jesus Christ!

HONORING WHO?

It would have been fascinating to be on the sidelines watching this exchange play out between Jesus and the Pharisees. Jesus brought no dishonor to the Father. Everything He did was 100 percent good. To accuse Him of honoring a different father—the devil—was so blasphemous. It was actually the Pharisees who dishonored the God they claimed to believe in.

If the Jews truly wanted to honor the Father in Heaven, they would also honor His Son, the Lord Jesus Christ. The Pharisees were convinced there was a demonic component to the miracles of Jesus, but no demon could ever perform the deeds of Jesus. The works they saw Him do were obviously from the hand of God and God alone. Their charge against Him was false. Everyone else could see it, but would they see it? The Pharisees missed the point that these miracles were God-sized encounters each time.

Another reason Jesus could not have an evil spirit is because evil spirits would never honor the Father. A devil would never utter the sayings He said, which we still use thousands of years later.

But the Pharisees were desperate. They were hurling a major accusation with no merit at Jesus because they were about to lose their prestige. They would no longer be at the top of the totem pole. Jesus came to turn things upside down, and they were fighting back.

> The days of visitation are come, the days of recompense are come; Israel shall know it: the prophet *is* a fool, the spiritual man *is* mad, for the multitude of thine iniquity, and the great hatred.
>
> **Hosea 9:7**

The religious leaders tried to accuse Jesus of being foolish, but it was actually the ones they saw looking back at them in the mirror each day who were the foolish ones. Their great hatred for the Son of God was obvious. God knew it, many of the people knew it, but they couldn't see it because their lust for power and control had blinded them.

> But he said, I am not mad, most noble Festus; but speak forth the words of truth and soberness. **Acts 26:25**

Paul was not mad and neither was Jesus, but the Pharisees were trying to make the accusation of lunacy stick. People might say you are crazy or have "gone off the deep end" because of your belief in Jesus, but do not forget that eternity is the final judge and not the people making those accusations.

Intentions matter to God as we live our lives. Jesus truly honored His Father, and that will be true for all of eternity. If He truly had a devil, He could not have honored the Father, spoken truth, performed miracles, or died for the sins of mankind.

These leaders were misreading the situation. Jesus is telling them He does not have a devil, and the works He is doing are of God. He is telling them His conscience is clear, but the real question before them was whether their consciences were clear.

SEEKING THE FATHER'S GLORY

God will judge all sin and evil, but He wants every Jew to be right with Him through Jesus. He wants them to honor His Son, and by doing so, they would be honoring Him.

> Jesus answered, If I honour myself, my honour is nothing: it is my Father that honoureth me; of whom ye say, that he is your God: **John 8:54**

> If I do not the works of my Father, believe me not. But if I do, though ye believe not me, believe the works: that ye may know, and believe, that the Father *is* in me, and I in him. **John 10:37,38**

Jesus continues to tell these leaders that it is God who is standing in front of them. He has confirmed it with His miraculous works and with His miraculous words. No one has ever done miracles like He has done, and no one has ever spoken words like He has spoken. But their hearts have been hardened.

They could come to Him—He is only a few steps away—but their unrepentant hearts won't let them make a move in His direction. Jesus is pulling out all the stops. He is giving them a massive amount of truth so they will make the right decision about His identity, but they refuse.

I receive not honour from men. **John 5:41**

He that speaketh of himself seeketh his own glory: but he that seeketh his glory that sent him, the same is true, and no unrighteousness is in him. **John 7:18**

If you don't worry about the praises of men, then you won't worry about the contempt of men either.

The great contrast taking place here is staggering. These religious men are seeking their own honor and glory. They are trying to protect the religious territory they think belongs to them. The new Man on the scene is stealing it from them, and they don't like it one bit. But interestingly, this new Man isn't worried about their approval. He doesn't seek the praises of men or seek His own glory—neither was on His agenda. He seeks only to please His Father and to gain the salvation of the world. Neither the Pharisees, nor anyone else, will get Him off track.

And immediately his fame spread abroad throughout all the region round about Galilee. **Mark 1:28**

There is a movement today among the youth to make Jesus famous across the world. Jesus is not looking for fame. He has already been famous. Fame is fleeting. Jesus is looking for us to share our faith and be bold soul winners for God. He is looking for people to repent and believe. Fame is futile and passing by the wayside, but the salvation of souls will last forever!

It is not good to eat much honey: so for men to search their own glory is not glory. **Proverbs 25:27**

If you don't worry about the praises of men, then you won't worry about the contempt of men either. Someone can mock you or your ministry, and it is really no big deal. Why? You aren't here to please people. You are here to please God alone.

> The wicked plotteth against the just, and gnasheth upon him with his teeth. The LORD shall laugh at him: for he seeth that his day is coming. The wicked have drawn out the sword, and have bent their bow, to cast down the poor and needy, *and* to slay such as be of upright conversation. Their sword shall enter into their own heart, and their bows shall be broken.   **Psalm 37:12-15**

I was reading an article recently about a cold-case murder. The murder happened 27 years ago. The police think they might be able to crack the case, but they don't realize it has already been solved. God knows who perpetrated the crime. Ultimately, people will not get away with breaking the law or mistreating others. The Righteous Judge knows all and will bring all things to light.

For those who dishonor Jesus and will not keep His Word, a day of reckoning is coming.

Those who do not honor the Lord, but mock Him, will not get away with their crimes either. They will be judged. God will turn their mocking right back on them, and it will not be a pretty sight. He is the totally impartial Judge who embodies all wisdom and knowledge, and these people will answer to Him one day, too. They just don't realize He is the man standing before them now.

KEEP MY WORD

For those who dishonor Jesus and will not keep His Word, a day of reckoning is coming. Mark that down. When it hits, there is no turning back.

> Verily, verily, I say unto you, He that heareth my word, and believeth on him that sent me, hath everlasting life, and shall not come into condemnation; but is passed from death unto life.   **John 5:24**

Then said Jesus to those Jews which believed on him, If ye continue in my word, *then* are ye my disciples indeed; **John 8:31**

These verses show us something very, very important. Keeping God's Word is huge to Him. It is near and dear to His heart. He is not wasting His words. He doesn't want His words to fall on barren ground. He wants people to hear and obey them. It's kind of simple when you think about it.

When Jesus says in verse 51 of our chapter's passage, "If a man keep my saying," He basically means *if a man keep My Word.* If you keep His Word, you will never see death. That is a profound statement. You may see the grave, but you will not see death! Again, He is making another claim to being God. He is able to back that up because, of course, He is God!

And for those who do keep His Word, they show that they love Him.

If ye love me, keep my commandments. **John 14:15**

He that hath my commandments, and keepeth them, he it is that loveth me: and he that loveth me shall be loved of my Father, and I will love him, and will manifest myself to him. **John 14:21**

If ye keep my commandments, ye shall abide in my love; even as I have kept my Father's commandments, and abide in his love.
John 15:10

Jesus answered and said unto him, If a man love me, he will keep my words: and my Father will love him, and we will come unto him, and make our abode with him. **John 14:23**

I have manifested thy name unto the men which thou gavest me out of the world: thine they were, and thou gavest them me; and they have kept thy word. **John 17:6**

That thou keep *this* commandment without spot, unrebukable, until the appearing of our Lord Jesus Christ: **1 Timothy 6:14**

You can't be a keeper of God's words unless you know God's words. Are you reading and studying your Bible on a daily basis? Remember, this isn't a race against the next person to see

who spends more time studying the Word of God. You answer to God and God alone. He is the only One who needs to be pleased with your life. Do not disregard the truths of God.

God's Word is also the ultimate defense before the jury of unbelievers. You can rest your case after you tell them the truth. And you tell them the truth because you care about them. Does truth matter to you so much that you want to tell the truths of God to anyone and everyone all the days of your life?

JUST PASSING THROUGH

In verse 51 of our chapter's passage, Jesus infers that death for the believer will not be eternal. We experience earthly death because the wages of sin is death, but we will live forever with God the Father, God the Son, and God the Holy Spirit because we have had a true born-again experience.

> For as in Adam all die, even so in Christ shall all be made alive. **1 Corinthians 15:22**

It is like having a ticket to a ball game. You already have the ticket. You are already going. You just have to show up. Once you arrive, you go through the metal detector, they scan your ticket, and you walk through the door. Same thing here.

There is no possibility of doubt in these words— true believers will never see death.

The born-again believer already has their ticket to Heaven. They just have to go through the door of death, leave their earthly body behind, and enjoy the King for all of eternity!

Since believers already have eternal life, *death* in this passage means something else. Believers are not going to see eternal death. There is no possibility of doubt in these words—true believers will never see death. We are just passing on through to the other side! We already have eternal life, and we will not lose it!

These things said he: and after that he saith unto them, Our friend Lazarus sleepeth; but I go, that I may awake him out of sleep.

John 11:11

So when this corruptible shall have put on incorruption, and this mortal shall have put on immortality, then shall be brought to pass  the saying that is written, Death is swallowed up in victory. O death, where *is* thy sting? O grave, where *is* thy victory? The sting of death *is* sin; and the strength of sin *is* the law. But thanks *be* to God, which giveth us the victory through our Lord Jesus Christ.

1 Corinthians 15:54-57

Scripture speaks of death as sleep that we wake up from on the other side.

Scripture speaks of death as sleep that we wake up from on the other side. It has been swallowed up in victory! Never, ever forget that. Jonah was swallowed up, but it wasn't a victory for him. Death for a believer is a great thing because they are delivered to Paradise for all of eternity! Death is the open door to the feet of Jesus. It is a great, grand, and awesome event for the believer! It is graduation day!

Therefore, when you pass from this life, death will have no power over you! The terror of death cannot truly affect you. It will be just a blip on the screen. One last breath here, and the next breath will be with the King on the other side! Death is just the doorway that opens to the throne that we all want to finally see! Hallelujah!!

Since believers have this hope, they are looking beyond death to bigger and better things. They know that real life isn't here; it's over there. They are looking for the Promised Land in Heaven. They are looking forward to leaving this worldly existence behind and taking their place with the Master at the wedding supper of the Lamb! Hallelujah!!

But please don't forget there is a second death for those who reject Jesus Christ. You want no one—and I do mean no one—to be in a lake that burns with fire and brimstone for all of eternity.

But the fearful, and unbelieving, and the abominable, and murderers, and whoremongers, and sorcerers, and idolaters, and all liars, shall have their part in the lake which burneth with fire and brimstone: which is the second death. **Revelation 21:8**

Neither can they die any more: for they are equal unto the angels; and are the children of God, being the children of the resurrection. **Luke 20:36**

Rather than seeking the true Messiah who offers them eternal life, the Jews were seeking a nationalistic Messiah who would take away the bondage of the Romans. They were seeking a better life now instead of eternal life forever! Look around you. Talk to people. They are in the same boat. They want to dress up this life and try to make it better when Jesus is trying to hand them the greatest gift of all—eternal life with Him!

We need to spend our lives serving the Lord! We need to reach the lost! Then we take our last breath and go enjoy Jesus for all of eternity!

So remember, we don't need to be hooked up to a bunch of machines at the end of our lives. We don't need tubes coming out of us. We don't need to spend our life's savings on the last few months of existence down here. We need to spend our lives serving the Lord! We need to reach the lost! Then we take our last breath and go enjoy Jesus for all of eternity!

But until that day arrives, we want to give all men the opportunity to believe on the Lord Jesus Christ to be saved. We want to give them truth. We want to dispel the lies they have learned from the world. And we want to warn them that if they don't heed His words, they will die in their sins. Either they believe that Jesus is God and believe His words, or they will join the ranks of unbelievers who mock God's truth and reap destruction forever. The eternal stakes are way too high to remain silent.

Chapter 9
Group Discussion

1. What did the Pharisees believe about their standing with God? How did their actions reveal they were following someone other than the Lord?

2. Why did Jesus confront and repeatedly warn the Pharisees about their unbelief and coming judgment? Explain why the Pharisees were fully able to repent and come to Jesus by faith.

3. When witnessing to the lost, do you ask them to explain their beliefs? Do you bring any false beliefs out in the open? What is at stake if their beliefs go unchallenged?

4. Compare some of the characteristics of the Pharisees with the characteristics of the Samaritans. What things made their hearts open or closed to truth? What did both groups need to believe to be saved?

5. When people resort to arguing with truth or name-calling, what does it reveal about their ability to defend their position? How important is using the Word in situations like these? What should you do if you find yourself on the receiving end of these types of accusations?

6. As you live your day-to-day life, whose honor and glory are you seeking and spreading? Would others agree with your self-assessment?

7. Give reasons why we should never seek the praises of men and why we should always seek the praises of God.

8. What does the unrepentant sinner have to look forward to at death? What does the believer look forward to at death? Why is it critically urgent to reach the lost now?

9. When we keep the sayings of Jesus, what does it say about our love and respect for Him? When we don't keep His Word, what does that also say about our love for and trust in God?

10. How sold out are you to the honor and glory of Jesus Christ? What evidences in your life show that you love the Lord with all your heart, mind, soul, and strength?

Matthew 8:23-27

And when he was entered into a ship,
his disciples followed him.

And, behold, there arose a great tempest in
the sea, insomuch that the ship was covered
with the waves: but he was asleep.

And his disciples came to *him,*
and awoke him, saying,
Lord, save us: we perish.

And he saith unto them, Why are ye fearful,
O ye of little faith? Then he arose,
and rebuked the winds and the sea;
and there was a great calm.

But the men marvelled, saying,
What manner of man is this,
that even the winds
and the sea obey him!

CHAPTER 10
Will You Take the Step of Faith?

OUT AT SEA

Putting together the parallel accounts in the gospels of Jesus calming the seas, we know it was evening, other boats were on the water, a fierce gale was blowing, waves were breaking over the ship, and Jesus was sleeping on a pillow!

This was just a simple fishing boat—no yacht, cruise ship, or steamliner for the Lord. He lived a regular person's life as He walked through His creation.

Fishermen know the sea can be dangerous. The apostles would have known that as well, but they followed Jesus out onto the open water anyway. Wherever He went, they went, too, which is certainly good advice for all of us. They might not have expected a storm to rise up while they were with Him, but they likely expected His protection wherever they went.

The Sea of Galilee has the reputation for violent storms that stir up suddenly. Winds come rushing down through the surrounding narrow mountain valleys causing great tempests to form quickly.

Interestingly, the imagery of winds and seas is often used to describe evil forces. Some believe the great gale that descended upon Jesus and His disciples could have possibly had satanic

origins. The prince of the power of the air might have thought Jesus was vulnerable in this small, wooden fishing boat. The evil one might have reasoned, *Some big waves and an unruly sea, and I can finally defeat Him!* He had his opening. Jesus was sleeping. Only one problem: Jesus is always aware of everything taking place! You know the devil is in trouble when he can't gain the advantage over the Son of God while He is sleeping! His best hope was that Jesus wouldn't wake up!

Being near to Jesus is always the best place to be.

The winds were howling. Waves were crashing over the ship and filling the vessel with water. It would be sinking soon. The apostles had real trouble on their hands, and, of course, Jesus was still sleeping!

> I will both lay me down in peace, and sleep: for thou, LORD, only makest me dwell in safety.
> **Psalm 4:8**

It kind of makes you wonder why the disciples didn't pull out a pillow and fall asleep, too. Being near to Jesus is always the best place to be. If He took His last breath that night, then they would take their last breath, as well. If Jesus survived this onslaught, then they would survive it, too.

Remember, Jesus could have prevented the storm, but He let the tempest descend upon them. This trial would show the disciples, one more time, that He is God.

CALLING ON THE NAME OF THE LORD

All of us have tempests in our lives, at one time or another, as we serve the Lord. They just go with the territory until our ship passes to the other side. But the disciples knew where to

go when trouble began. By the way, who do you run to the moment trouble first appears? Are you busy running to the police, doctors, counselors, pastors, and friends, or do you run to the only One who can truly get you out of trouble?

Even though Jesus slept as the tempest raged, He was always in control. So when you have one of those tempest-tossing struggles going on in your life, you can rest easy because Jesus is more in control than you can ever imagine.

It's interesting to consider what might have been running through the apostles' minds as the storm worsened. Did they debate about letting Jesus continue to sleep? *Don't bother Him. He is resting. No worries. He will awake in time to take care of us.* Or did they reason among themselves, *Since this appears to be no big deal to Him, this shouldn't be a big deal to us?* Or did they see that the boat was taking on water and think, *If we don't wake Him up now, this boat is going to capsize, and we will certainly die!!*

So when you have one of those tempest-tossing struggles going on in your life, you can rest easy because Jesus is more in control than you can ever imagine.

In Mark's gospel, the apostles woke Jesus by asking a surprising question: "Master, carest thou not that we perish?" They knew He cared for them. He wasn't taking a day off from His concern for them, but panic was setting in. They must have wondered if Jesus was indifferent to their circumstances because, after all, He was sleeping.

Since some of the disciples were experienced fishermen, they wouldn't have cried out for help unless they were in dire circumstances. Typically, they could handle whatever weather moved across the sea, but this storm was different. Death was upon them, and they knew it. By this point, they were screaming for help. They needed Jesus to come to their rescue immediately—*Lord, save us!*

And it shall come to pass, *that* whosoever shall call on the name of the Lord shall be saved.   **Acts 2:21**

So ask yourself, who would you cry out to if death were at your door? Whenever we face serious circumstances, we must fervently call on the right Person to save us! There is no hope of true help unless we cry out for Jesus to answer our prayers. And even though in this situation He was sleeping, as eternal God, He never sleeps or slumbers.

CALMING THE SEA

Never forget that when tempests arise in your life, Jesus can bring complete peace to those situations. In this case, He first

calmed the hearts of the disciples; then He stopped the winds—and there was great calm. A total hurricane had been stirring things up, but now there was total peace on the lake. The miracle was instantaneous.

The forces of nature were easy for Jesus to handle; it is humans who are an unruly bunch.

Notice that Jesus rebuked the winds and the sea. Ellicott's Commentary makes some interesting observations about this command: "This seems to have been almost, so to say, our Lord's formula in working miracles. The fever (Luke 4:39), the frenzy of the demoniac (Mark 9:25), the tempest, are all treated as if they were hostile and rebel forces that needed to be restrained. St. Mark, with his usual vividness, gives the very words of the rebuke: 'Peace, be still'—literally, be dumb, be muzzled, as though the howling wind was a maniac to be gagged and bound."[40]

The forces of nature were easy for Jesus to handle; it is humans who are an unruly bunch. And if this was a demonically inspired storm and if demons were behind the wind, Jesus was able to overpower their attack in an instant. He rebuked them because He was fully able to do so! He is in complete control at all times. He gave the command, and it was done.

WHERE IS YOUR FAITH?

After stilling the storm, Jesus wanted to know from the apostles where was their faith during this trial. Faith implies placing complete trust and confidence in something or someone. He didn't rebuke the disciples for waking him, but He did rebuke them for their little faith. They should have trusted Him. They should have had full confidence in Him. Little faith is so dishonoring to the Lord. Faith should always be bold and never timid. Since God is great, He is worthy of great faith as well.

> And the apostles said unto the Lord, Increase our faith. **Luke 17:5**

> Then they cry unto the LORD in their trouble, and he bringeth them out of their distresses. He maketh the storm a calm, so that the waves thereof are still.
> **Psalm 107:28,29**

Always remember that fear and unbelief go hand in hand. But when we walk hand in hand with faith in the One who is worthy of our trust, fear just falls by the wayside.

Trials can be some of the most amazing times in our lives. They increase our faith and teach us to trust the Lord no matter what the circumstance is.

The apostles should have known that Jesus would always come through for them. By this time, they had seen Him perform great miracles, so they should have been walking in faith rather than in doubt. Not only should they have known better by then, we should know better, too. As we grow older in the Lord, our faith should become stronger and stronger. Those around us should notice the strength of our faith, too. Always remember that fear and unbelief go hand in hand. But when we walk hand in hand with faith in the One who is worthy of our trust, fear just falls by the wayside.

MARVELING AT THE MIRACLE

When storms pass across the sea, the waters continue to be tumultuous until the bad weather has cleared. But Jesus brought immediate calm as He spoke to His creation and silenced the gale.

> Which stilleth the noise of the seas, the noise of their waves, and the tumult of the people. **Psalm 65:7**

The mariners who followed Jesus out to sea witnessed firsthand how the tempest had become instantly quiet. Had the water become a glassy sea? Had everything become completely peaceful? Were their voices echoing across the water as they expressed awe over the miracle they had just witnessed? One thing we know, when the wind and the waves obeyed Jesus' command, they all marveled and wondered who He might really be.

Jesus brought immediate calm as He spoke to His creation and silenced the gale.

> Fear thou not; for I *am* with thee: be not dismayed; for I *am* thy God: I will strengthen thee; yea, I will help thee; yea, I will uphold thee with the right hand of my righteousness. Behold, all they that were incensed against thee shall be ashamed and confounded: they shall be as nothing; and they that strive with thee shall perish. Thou shalt seek them, and shalt not find them, *even* them that contended with thee: they that war against thee shall be as nothing, and as a thing of nought. For I the LORD thy God will hold thy right hand, saying unto thee, Fear not; I will help thee. Fear not, thou worm Jacob, *and* ye men of Israel; I will help thee, saith the LORD, and thy redeemer, the Holy One of Israel. **Isaiah 41:10-14**

These experienced seamen, who had navigated the open waters for years, had never seen anything like this before. Jesus had stilled the seas, and now they were just as still as they understood that Someone very special was in their midst.

Marveling about the miracle was a good thing, but they faced the same question that faces all men today: *What will we do with the One who performed these miracles?*

Who hath ascended up into heaven, or descended? who hath gathered the wind in his fists? who hath bound the waters in a garment? who hath established all the ends of the earth? what *is* his name, and what *is* his son's name, if thou canst tell?

Proverbs 30:4

Jesus was showing that He is God manifest in the flesh.

The power that Jesus exerts over the laws of nature testifies to His identity. His supremacy shouts over the chatter and lies of men to grab their attention. They need to consider who they are in the light of who He really is.

The heavens declare the glory of God; and the firmament sheweth his handywork. Day unto day uttereth speech, and night unto night sheweth knowledge.   **Psalm 19:1,2**

"Every part of the creation (man excepted) hears and obeys the Creator's voice. Sinners have an ear for the world, the devil, and the flesh: till this ear is shut, God's voice is not discerned; for when it is shut to its enemies it is open to its friends."[41]

This miracle spoke volumes to all who witnessed it. Jesus was showing that He is God manifest in the flesh. The disciples had no idea He possessed this kind of power. All who witnessed this miracle take place were overcome by the implications of what they had just seen! This storm provided the opportunity for some of His power to come forward, which proved beyond a shadow of a doubt that He is God incarnate. And if He is truly God, then He *should* have power over the realm of nature. After all, He created it in the first place!

Who laid the foundations of the earth, *that* it should not be removed for ever. Thou coveredst it with the deep as *with* a garment: the waters stood above the mountains. At thy rebuke they fled; at the

voice of thy thunder they hasted away. They go up by the mountains; they go down by the valleys unto the place which thou hast founded for them.
Psalm 104:5-8

O L ORD God of hosts, who *is* a strong L ORD like unto thee? or to thy faithfulness round about thee? Thou rulest the raging of the sea: when the waves thereof arise, thou stillest them.
Psalm 89:8,9

Jesus strengthens the faith of those who are faint of heart and quiets the storms they face.

We don't want to miss the application for the church today. Those who have repented and believed the gospel are in the boat with Christ. They suffer the winds of persecution that try to thwart the spread of the gospel, but Jesus always hears the cries of those who suffer for His name's sake. He strengthens the faith of those who are faint of heart and quiets the storms they face. One thing we know is that the gates of Hell will never prevail against the church. The boat carrying truth to this lost and dying world has been sailing through history and will arrive safely on the distant shore of Heaven when the work of God's people is done.

The apostles saw Jesus sleeping in His humanity, and they saw Jesus overpowering creation in His divinity. They were eye-witnesses of the One who is truly man and truly God!

Trust ye in the L ORD for ever: for in the L ORD JEHOVAH is everlasting strength:
Isaiah 26:4

Fear ye not me? saith the L ORD: will ye not tremble at my presence, which have placed the sand *for* the bound of the sea by a perpetual decree, that it cannot pass it: and though the waves thereof toss themselves, yet can they not prevail; though they roar, yet can they not pass over it?
Jeremiah 5:22

So there is no need to fear as you reach everyone you can while you can for the Lord Jesus Christ. There is no need to

fear men as you boldly proclaim that He died for the sins of the world. He is with you wherever you go, and He can quiet every storm with just a word. That is the power of our God!

PEBBLE IN YOUR SHOE

As we bring this book to a close, I'd like to recall what a friend of mine, Dave, has always said: "Death is a comma, not a period." The journey continues on the other side for all of us.

But his statement also begs a question that we should not only be asking of ourselves but one that was asked 2,000 years ago by the Philippian jailer in Acts 16:30: "…Sirs, what must I do to be saved?"

Only those who are born again will see the Kingdom of Heaven (John 3:3). If you have not repented of your sins and believed upon the Lord Jesus Christ for the forgiveness of those sins, then today is the day of salvation for you. You need to get saved today. Don't put your head on your pillow tonight until you know for sure where you will spend eternity. Never waste your life, and make sure to never waste your eternal life.

Just like a pebble or a rock can send ripples all the way across a lake, the effects of a good question can ripple through all of eternity as well!

When you ask a good question, as we mentioned in the introduction of this book, it can have that pebble-in-your-shoe effect. But another good thing to keep in mind is that just like a pebble or a rock can send ripples all the way across a lake, the effects of a good question can ripple through all of eternity as well!

I was walking out of a hotel one day and saw a man standing there smoking a cigarette. I handed him a gospel tract as I was heading toward my car to drive to a speaking event. But I knew deep down I was supposed to do more than just hand him a tract; I was supposed to talk with him. So I did a U-turn and went back. I have done many U-turns in my life. I have even done U-turns with my car to go back and talk to people! Remember, if you pass up someone who you know you are supposed to talk with, just do a U-turn and go back to them. You won't regret it, and neither will they!

Think about what God cannot do because a seed has not been planted.

When I walked up to the guy, I said, "Can I ask you an interesting question?" He said, "Sure." When I asked if he were to die that night and was he 100 percent sure that he would go to Heaven, he responded by saying, "Yes." I asked, "How do you know that to be true?" Well, he started preaching to me! He had a real strong relationship with Jesus Christ. So I challenged him to be bold in reaching the lost, gave him a book, and started walking away. Then he called me back and said, "Before you go, can I say something to you?" As I walked back toward him, he explained that thirty years ago one of his coworkers asked him the exact same question! He told the man he wasn't interested. His answer didn't fluster that Christian man in the least, who replied that if he ever wanted to talk about it, to let him know. Well three years later, this guy knocked on the Christian man's door and asked if he could come in and talk. The Christian man replied, "Come on in and have a seat. I know what you want to talk about!" That man already knew he wanted to talk about Jesus. This guy told me that he thought about his coworker's question—*If you died tonight, are you 100 percent sure you would go to Heaven*—every single day for three straight years! Wow!! His coworker just planted a seed with him and had no clue what God would do with that seed! We also have no idea what God will do with the seeds we plant. Conversely, think about what God cannot do because a seed has not been planted. That's right, nothing!

CHAPTER 10

So continue to be seed planters for the Lord in the days to come. And never forget about the ripple effect that can be set in motion by asking one good question.

As I was putting this book together, I received an email from a friend of mine. Jon reminded me of a witnessing encounter I had one time in Alabama. He wrote:

> The guy you met at the gas station near my clinic ten years ago, who was up on murder charges—Jeep, Auburn decal on the back of the spare tire—he came to Flint Hill Baptist Church to hear you speak on a Sunday night seven years ago, after he ended up in my clinic two weeks before you came. That was the same weekend Brittney and I had dinner with you at J. Alexander's near the mall.

> He gave his life to Jesus that night after he heard you speak at FHBC. He ended up doing a year in prison for manslaughter. Later, I ended up preaching at Brandon's attorney's funeral (who was also a patient of mine), and I gave out about 120 *One Heartbeat Away* books and met his mom and sister at the end of the funeral. His mom couldn't pray for him for months because she was mad at God. You contacted her one day to check on him, and you encouraged her to start praying for him, which she did at 1 p.m. that day. She told Brandon that you had encouraged her to pray for him, and she started praying at 1 p.m. He told her that exactly as she was praying at 1 p.m., he was in his cell and found one of your books. He had not seen any books of yours in the entire prison before that moment, and they weren't even allowed to have any books in the cells. He was so encouraged.

I definitely remember the encounter at the gas station. I had pulled in to fill up my tank before driving back to Atlanta. No one was at any of the pumps! I prayed for God to have someone drive up so I could talk with them. Well, Brandon and his friend pulled up in that Jeep! As we started talking, Brandon looked at his friend and said, "Should we tell him?" His friend answered in the affirmative, so he told me about the situation that caused the murder charges to be brought up against him, and the rest will just ripple into eternal history.

Great Company

> The Lord gave the word: great *was* the company of those that published *it.*
>
> **Psalm 68:11**

Remember that evangelism is something the Lord commands of all Christians! We are the *great company* of Psalm 68 who *publish*, meaning to "proclaim" or "broadcast," the gospel!

We received another email at the ministry not long ago from someone who is of the *great company:*

> The Holy Spirit used your words on your DVD the other day to really speak to my heart.
>
> Speaking of witnessing, you said it was "our job." Wow! I had looked at witnessing as a choice, which, of course, it is, but what if, when I was working as an employee at a company, I treated my job as carelessly as I have witnessing?
>
> What if I decided I didn't want to go to work because I didn't feel like it? I would be fired! What if I was going to school, and I didn't feel like studying? I would flunk!
>
> I started thinking, *How dare I, a child of God, who was saved through His Son's blood shed for my sins, and given the hope of heaven for my future, treat His command to share the gospel to others so carelessly and casually.*
>
> I now look at witnessing as "my job," too! I know I have a long way to go, but I am even more committed to treating this as my priority now!

Remember that evangelism is something the Lord commands of all Christians!

I hope you have enjoyed this book and the teachings we have included. But now, it is time to put the book down and join the *great company* who publishes the gospel. It is time to follow the example of the King, who asked great questions of the lost 2,000 years ago and asks great things of you today. Will you do your part to make sure that the Lord's house is full?

> "To every lost soul, Christ says: Come unto Me.
> To every redeemed soul, Christ says: Go for Me."
> **—Unknown**

Now that you have learned some questions from the Master, the next step is to put them into practice. You have been given today, and most of us will have many more tomorrows to live here on Earth. Will we spend those days on the things of the world? Or will the impact of our lives reverberate throughout all of eternity because we used it mightily for the King? God has given us the honor of declaring His name openly to the world. Do we realize that He has put His priceless treasure—the gospel of salvation—in the hands of His saints? He has vested us with His trust to faithfully explain the gospel to the lost. Dare we let that treasure be hidden away or kept from shedding its light in the world? There is no greater calling, higher privilege, more solemn responsibility, or thrilling joy in life than giving ourselves fully to the Lord for Him to use. Living entirely for Christ is a decision you get to make, and you will not regret it either here or for all of eternity. Will you stand up for Him on the highways and byways of life today? What choice will you make in the next minute, hour, day, and week? Your tomorrows are rushing toward you. The day you will stand before the King will be here quicker than you think. Time to close the book, open your mouth, and go ask and answer great questions all the days of your life!

Time to close the book, open your mouth, and go ask and answer great questions all the days of your life!

Chapter 10
Group Discussion

1. Recount a time when you trusted the Lord and stepped out in faith only to be met by a tremendous storm. What problems stirred up unexpectedly? For what did you trust the Lord? What was the outcome in the end?

2. When the storms of life come seemingly out of nowhere, what are your first thoughts? Who is the first person you seek or the first place you turn for help?

3. Name a time when you went through a severe trial. What tests of faith did you face? What prayers did you offer up to the Lord? How did He meet your cry for mercy? What was the outcome of that test of faith?

4. Whom do you most trust or fear in life and why? How can you lead by example so others properly place their trust in the Lord?

5. What example is set for others when you actively trust the Lord? What example is set for them when you fear your circumstances? Name some of the blessings or repercussions that come when others follow your example.

6. What authority and control does Jesus have over the forces of nature or the realm of evil? How confident can we be that He is able to answer our prayers? Name a time when He did the impossible in response to your prayers.

7. Describe the immensity of God and His character. How worthy is He of our trust? How does little faith and great faith reflect on the Lord?

8. Explain the impact the Lord has made on the lost through your faithful witness to them. Who has come to salvation because you communicated the truth of the gospel to them? How can their salvation ripple through their circumstances and into the lives of others?

9. What job has God given Christians today? What can God do with a seed that is planted? What can God not do with a seed that is not planted? When the gospel is not preached, how are the lost, the saved, and the Lord affected?

10. What is holding you back from reaching the lost? Are you ready to step outside of your comfort zone and begin stepping out in faith? List the benefits for you, the Lord, and others if you will start reaching the lost today.

Endnotes

1 Mark Chernoff, *"50 Questions That Will Free Your Mind,"* *<http://www.marcandangel.com/2009/07/13/50-questions-that-will-free-your-mind/>*

2 Ibid.

3 Bob Bishop, *"Humorous Questions That Make You Think Twice-Part #1" <https://motivationalmagic.wordpress.com/2009/09/08/humorous-questions-that-make-you-think-twice/>*

4 Rick Wayne, *"Top Ten Greatest Philosophical Questions of All Time," <http://rickwayne.com/top-10-greatest-philosophical-questions-of-all-time/>*

5 Napoleon Bonaparte, *<https://www.quotedb.com/quotes/2505>*

6 Mahatma Gandhi, *< www.famous-quotes.com/topic.php?tid=676>*

7 John Lennon, *<www.brainyquote.com/quotes/authors/j/john_lennon.html>*

8 Thomas Jefferson in a letter to John Adams (4/11/1823), *< http://www.beliefnet.com/resourcelib/docs/53/Letter_from_Thomas_Jefferson_to_John_Adams_1.html>*

9 H. G. Wells, *<http://www.tentmaker.org/Quotes/jesus-christ.htm>*

10 Peter Larson, *< http://www.finestquotes.com/author_quotes-author-Peter+Larson-page-0.htm>*

11 Elton John to Parade Magazine, *<www.popeater.com/2010/02/18/elton-johnjesus-gay/>*

12 Benjamin Franklin, *<http://quotes.liberty-tree.ca/quote_blog/Benjamin.Franklin.Quote.1D11>*

13 Albert Einstein, *<http://voice-wilderness.org/quotes-about-god/einstein-on-life/>*

14 Larry King, *<www.tentmaker.org/Quotes/jesus-christ.htm>*

15 Steve Bauer, *The Math of Christ,* (Crane, MO: Defender Publishing, 2010) p. 21

16 Ibid., p. 94-95

17 Ibid., p. 95.

18 Ibid., p. 96

19 Ibid., p. 120.

20 *<http://www.dictionary.com/browse/cornerstone>*

21 Adam Clarke, *Adam Clarke Commentary,* Matthew 21:42, *<http://biblehub.com/commentaries/clarke/matthew/21.htm>*

22 Ibid., Matthew 21:44.

23 Horace Greeley, <http://www. goodreads.com/quotes/117998-it-is-impossible-to-enslave-mentally-or-socially-a-bible-reading>

24 William Gladstone, <http://www. thescriptures.org/quotes/>

25 Andrew Jackson, <https://wall-builders.com/read-the-bible/>

26 Henri Nouwen, *Sabbatical Journey* (New York, NY: Crossroad Publishing Company, 1998), p. 51.

27 Matthew Henry, *Matthew Henry Commentary,* Matthew 12:33, <http://biblehub.com/commentaries/mhc/matthew/12.htm>

28 Winston Churchill, <http://www. brainyquote.com/quotes/quotes/w/winstonchu135210.html>

29 Clarke, *Adam Clarke Commentary,* Matthew 23:37, <http://biblehub.com/commentaries/clarke/matthew/23.htm>

30 Ibid.

31 C. T. Studd, <http://www. goodreads.com/quotes/715176-if-jesus-christ-be-god-and-died-for-me-then>

32 Clarke, *Adam Clarke Commentary,* Luke 15:4, <http://biblehub.com/commentaries/clarke/luke/15.htm>

33 *Expositor's Bible Commentary,* <http://biblehub.com/commentaries/expositors/luke/15.htm>

34 David Cloud, <http://www.wayoflife.org/reports/evidences_of_salvation.html>

35 David Cloud, "Paul's Doctrine of Repentance," *Friday Church News Notes,* May 20, 2016, <https://www.wayoflife.org/pdf/20160520.pdf>

36 David Cloud, "Contemporary Christian Music and Homosexuality," <http://www.wayoflife.org/database/ccm_and_homosexuality.php>

37 Adam Clarke, *Adam Clarke Commentary,* Luke12:59, <http://biblehub.com/commentaries/clarke/luke/12.htm>

38 Charles Ellicott, *Ellicott's Commentary,* John 8:26, <http://biblehub.com/commentaries/ellicott/john/8.htm >

39 Charles Ellicott, *Ellicott's Commentary for English Readers,* John 8:48, <http://biblehub.com/commentaries/john/8.htm>

40 Ibid, Matthew 8:26, <http://biblehub.com/commentaries/matthew/8.htm>

41 Clarke, *Adam Clarke Commentary,* Matthew 8:27, <http://biblehub.com/commentaries/clarke/matthew/8.htm>

EVANGELISM RESOURCES

MARK CAHILL MINISTRIES

www.markcahill.org

Mark Cahill has a business degree from Auburn University, where he was an honorable mention Academic All-American in basketball. He has worked in the business world at IBM and in various management positions, and he taught high school for four years. Mark now speaks to thousands of people a year at churches, retreats, conferences, camps, and other events. He has also appeared on numerous radio and television shows.

Mark's favorite thing to do is to go out and meet people to find out not only what they believe but why they believe it. You can find Mark at malls, concerts, art and music festivals, airports, beaches, sporting events, bar sections of towns, college campuses, and wherever people gather, doing just that.

To arrange a speaking engagement, contact:
Ambassador Agency
615-370-4700
www.ambassadoragency.com

•

Contact Mark Cahill at:
P.O. Box 81, Stone Mountain, GA 30086
800-NETS-158 / mark@markcahill.org

•

To order additional books or
other **evangelism materials,** or
to receive a free e-newsletter, visit:
www.markcahill.org